The Tempest

The Shakespeare Workbook Series

The Tempest

The Shakespeare Workbook Series

Commentary by
John Russell Brown and Neil Freeman

Edited by Paul Sugarman

BLOOMSBURY ACADEMIC
NEW YORK • LONDON • OXFORD • NEW DELHI • SYDNEY

BLOOMSBURY ACADEMIC

Bloomsbury Publishing Inc, 1359 Broadway, 12th Floor, New York, NY 10018, USA
Bloomsbury Publishing Plc, 50 Bedford Square, London, WC1B 3DP, UK
Bloomsbury Publishing Ireland, 29 Earlsfort Terrace, Dublin 2, D02 AY28, Ireland
BLOOMSBURY, BLOOMSBURY ACADEMIC and the Diana logo are trademarks of Bloomsbury Publishing Plc

First published in the United States of America 2026

Copyright © Bloomsbury Publishing, 2026

Material drawn from *Shakescenes: Shakespeare for Two*
Copyright © 1992 Applause Theatre Book Publishers

Material drawn from *Once More Unto the Speech Dear Friends*
Copyright © 2006 Folio Scripts, Vancouver, Canada

Material drawn from *The Tempest: The Applause Shakespeare Library*
Copyright © 1996 Applause Books

Introduction and other additional material © 2026 Paul Sugarman

Cover design: Chloe Batch

All rights reserved. No part of this publication may be: i) reproduced or transmitted in any form, electronic or mechanical, including photocopying, recording or by means of any information storage or retrieval system without prior permission in writing from the publishers; or ii) used or reproduced in any way for the training, development or operation of artificial intelligence (AI) technologies, including generative AI technologies. The rights holders expressly reserve this publication from the text and data mining exception as per Article 4(3) of the Digital Single Market Directive (EU) 2019/790.

Bloomsbury Publishing Inc does not have any control over, or responsibility for, any third-party websites referred to or in this book. All internet addresses given in this book were correct at the time of going to press. The author and publisher regret any inconvenience caused if addresses have changed or sites have ceased to exist, but can accept no responsibility for any such changes.

Library of Congress Cataloging-in-Publication Data Available
Library of Congress Control Number: 2026931372

ISBN: PB: 978-1-4930-5710-8
ePDF: 979-8-7651-5543-1
eBook: 978-1-4930-5711-5

Typeset by Amnet

For product safety related questions contact productsafety@bloomsbury.com.
To find out more about our authors and books visit www.bloomsbury.com and sign up for our newsletters.

CONTENTS

Introduction by Paul Sugarman 7

Original Practices and Cue Scripts by Paul Sugarman 11

Advice to Actors by John Russell Brown 14

Brief Background to the First Folio by Neil Freeman 31

Scene Study: Act II, Scene i (Sebastian and Antonio) 43

Working on Modern and First Folio Texts 53

    Act I, Scene ii (Prospero, Miranda, Ariel) 54

    Act II, Scene i (Gonzalo, Sebastian, Antonio) 68

    Act II, Scene ii (Caliban, Trinculo) 74

    Act III, Scene i (Ferdinand, Miranda, Prospero) 82

    Act III, Scene ii (Caliban) 98

    Act IV, Scene i (Prospero, Ferdinand, Miranda) 102

OVERVIEW: WORKING ON SHAKESPEARE TO BUILD TOWARD PERFORMANCE

Perform the Text: Share the text with a wider audience.

Share the Text: Speak the text to someone else.

Action: Find the Choices in the Text: What choices can be made in terms of the character?

Explore the Text: Consult the First Folio to see how capitalization, punctuation, and line endings can shift emphasis. Connect to the text physically and personally.

Analyze the Text: Look at the text in depth to see how it works. Is it verse or prose?

Understand the Text: You need to understand what is being said and what all the words mean.

Read the Text Aloud: These words were meant to be spoken.

INTRODUCTION

Paul Sugarman

The aim of this Applause Shakespeare Workbook is to provide tools for working on the text of *The Tempest*. Out of the many Bloomsbury publications on Shakespeare this book draws material from the works of John Russell Brown (*Shakescenes* and the Applause Shakespeare Library) and Neil Freeman (*Once More Unto the Speech* series and the Folio Texts) to give you and/or your actors or students practical approaches to work on the text.

These plays, while they speak much to our human condition today, are from more than four hundred years ago. To fully appreciate Shakespeare, there is a lot that one needs to know. There are many books published by Bloomsbury that can help you understand and work on Shakespeare. First you need to understand the time when he lived, which has similarities to today and many differences. *William Shakespeare: A Popular Life* by Garry O'Connor gives insight into Shakespeare's time. Much like Stephen Greenblatt's *Will in the World*, it paints a picture of Shakespeare's age and makes connections between that time and the text in his plays that give a broader perspective on the images and references in Shakespeare's works.

There is the need for much more in-depth study and work on how to use your voice to speak the text. Bloomsbury publishes *The Actor and the Text* by Cicely Berry, which reveals how Shakespeare uses language to express so much in such a wide variety of ways and the need to have a strong and connected voice to be able to do it justice. She includes hands-on approaches to the text to show how Shakespeare uses rhetoric to make his points. Her *Working Shakespeare* video series shows many top UK and US actors putting her techniques into practice.

There is also the practicality of how to understand his work in performance. One of John Russell Brown's central ideas is that you can't fully understand and appreciate Shakespeare without understanding how it works in performance. He wrote many books on Shakespeare and many editions of the works of Shakespeare and other early modern playwrights. Bloomsbury publishes many of his books including

Shakescenes, which provides material for this book; and *Shakespeare's Plays in Performance*, which looks at performance elements and performance history. *Free Shakespeare* contrasts how the plays were originally performed with the vision of the actor-based ensembles, which has been influential for many American acting companies. John Russell Brown created the Applause Shakespeare Library, which included theatrical commentary to make sure that performance considerations are an essential part of studying the play. There is also much that can be gained from great performers of Shakespeare as shown by John Gielgud's books *Acting Shakespeare* and *An Actor and His Time*, as well as the many fine biographies of great stage actors such as Gielgud, Laurence Olivier, and Ralph Richardson, also published by Bloomsbury.

The importance of the first collected publication of Shakespeare's plays, the First Folio of 1623, cannot be underestimated. It collected thirty-six of Shakespeare's plays, eighteen of which had never been published before and would have been lost forever. Bloomsbury publishes all thirty-six plays from the First Folio in individual editions that were prepared and annotated by Neil Freeman. Bloomsbury publishes the single volume *The Applause First Folio of Shakespeare in Modern Type*. Freeman then went on to create the *Once More Unto the Speech* series of books comparing modern and Folio texts for more than nine hundred speeches, demonstrating the practicality of using Folio texts. Material from that series has been made more accessible in the recent series of *Monologues from Shakespeare's First Folio* series of twelve books. Neil Freeman was one of the major forces in making the First Folio more useful for actors and students of the plays.

Both John Russell Brown and Neil Freeman were champions for understanding Shakespeare through performance. John Russell Brown's Applause Shakespeare Library was designed to make one aware of the many opportunities presented by the text for performance. Neil Freeman's First Folio texts showed the many clues and choices that could be explored through looking at the text as originally printed. By taking examples from both men's work, these materials present different perspectives on the text.

The wonderful thing about working on Shakespeare is that there is no one "right" answer. His work endures because it is so flexible and subject to varied interpretations. In your own exploration of the text you have to find which choices work best for you (and, perhaps, your students). To find the best choice you need to explore what is out there and why these more than four-hundred-year-old texts still speak to us today.

This workbook presents a brief description of various approaches to the text by John Russell Brown and Neil Freeman. Following are scenes from the play that John Russell Brown had included in *Shakescenes* along with further selections from the Applause Shakespeare Library edition of the play. Speeches from the play drawn from Neil Freeman's *Once More Unto the Speech* series will give a First Folio perspective on the text.

The goal is to be able to speak and share Shakespeare's words in a way that makes the plays come alive in ways they do not when read silently. Perhaps the biggest perceived challenge is understanding and getting comfortable with Shakespeare's language. Though the language may seem old to us, the English language of Shakespeare was four hundred years *younger* then than it is now, as Kristin Linklater, author of *Freeing Shakespeare's Voice*, observed. Although these words are from four centuries ago, it is still Modern English but in its infancy, when it was still blossoming and expanding. The spoken word was essential to almost all communication in Shakespeare's day, unlike our predominantly visual and text-based age. We don't talk as much or as precisely as those whose lives depended on spoken communication in Shakespeare's time. Shakespeare does a lot more with language than we do in our modern world. Working on Shakespeare's language can open one up to new and more effective ways of communicating. These great thoughts and words show the possibilities of expression that a human voice can achieve.

Basic Steps to Working on Shakespeare's Text

Read the Text Aloud: These words were meant to be spoken. Music cannot be experienced solely by looking at annotations on a page. Neither can Shakespeare.

Understand the Text: You need to understand what is being said and what all the words mean. It is important to consult glossaries that give Elizabethan definitions and context. David and Ben Crystal's website shakespeareswords.com is a good place to start.

Analyze the Text: Look at the text in depth to see how it works. Is it verse or prose? If verse, where is it regular and where not? Shakespeare uses rhetorical devices to convey feelings and meanings. How do the sounds and words "play" off each other?

Explore the Text: Consult the First Folio to see how capitalization, punctuation, and line endings can shift emphasis. Connect to the text physically and personally. How do the words and sounds feel inside your body?

Action: Find the Choices in the Text: What choices can be made in terms of the character? What actions can they take? What choices can be made about their needs? Some choices may seem obvious, but look for the possibilities of different ones.

Share the Text: Speak the text to someone else so that you can assess how well you are communicating the thoughts beneath the text.

Perform the Text: Share the text with a wider audience, to whom you can also speak directly, as there was no fourth wall in Shakespeare's theater.

Committing to speaking Shakespeare's text requires more of us than most contemporary communication does. Energize the whole body when giving voice to the text. There have been many fine books on using the voice to support Shakespeare text work including *The Actor and the Text* by Cicely Berry (Applause) and *Freeing Shakespeare's Voice* by Kristin Linklater (TCG).

The exploration of the text can continue indefinitely as there is no one answer to these texts but an endless array of possibilities to be explored. However, if you start with speaking and listening instead of just reading the words, it will lead you to a more personal connection to the text.

Shakespeare connects to so many people in different ways because we find something in our personal lives that is explained by the way Shakespeare says it. Sometimes the text instantly makes sense to you, but often the possibilities are infinite. We make choices based on how the text connects to us at this moment in our time.

This workbook will outline some of the tools to look at the text and give examples from the works of John Russell Brown and Neil Freeman, who can offer differing viewpoints on the same text as a way for you to learn to trust your ear and your connection to the text. This workbook will show ways to work on the text with a spirit of exploration.

ORIGINAL PRACTICES AND CUE SCRIPTS

Paul Sugarman

What do we know of the original practices of Shakespeare's time? Most of the evidence we have comes from Philip Henslowe, who was the owner of the Rose Theatre. His "diary," which was a log book of receipts for shows that they would perform 6 days a week, including many different plays. In a month where they could do 24–27 performances they would stage 15–20 different plays with only a few repeated more than once. We have little documentation on the rehearsal and performance practices of the time, but we are able to get an idea of how they worked from references in plays (such as the Mechanicals rehearsals in *A Midsummer Night's Dream*) and the papers left by Edward Alleyn, Henslowe's son-in-law and the lead actor of The Lord Admiral's Men.

Edward Alleyn was, along with Richard Burbage, one of the leading actors of Shakespeare's time. Alleyn founded Dulwich College, to which he bequeathed papers from his theatrical career, including Henslowe's diary, a cue script from *Orlando Furioso* and a platt (scene plot) for *The Seven Deadlie Sinnes* from which scholars have deduced what we know of the rehearsal practices of the day. Instead of receiving the full text, the actors would get a cue script which had their lines and the line that came before their line (their cue). A platt was a listing of all the scenes with entrances and sound cues that would be hung backstage for the cast to refer to.

The cue scripts were hand-written by copyists. By just giving the actors their lines and cues it was easier for the company than providing a whole script. Also, it allowed the company to maintain tighter control over the complete text of a play since copyright didn't really exist back then. If a rival company of actors got hold of a play text there would be nothing to stop them from performing it. Full scripts were kept under lock and key at the theatre.

Cue scripts have enjoyed something of a renaissance with Patrick Tucker (another contemporary champion of the First Folio). The Original Shakespeare Company created by Tucker did performances using scrolls with very minimal rehearsal to mimic the conditions under which the plays might usually have been done.

A number of Shakespeare companies work with cue scripts. Cue script Shakespeare performances have been presented by many companies that did readings from scrolls, including the Actors Shakespeare Company and Spontaneous Shakespeare. For readings they are quite useful as they are compact enough that one can move easily with them and it can look more like a performance than a reading in which actors are carrying around conspicuous scripts.

They are very useful for learning lines, as you can focus solely on your cues, dialogue, and speeches. They are convenient to carry around. There are a number of actors who have told me that they set up cue scripts when they're doing contemporary plays as well, as they are just a useful mechanism for learning lines. In Shakespeare's time, scrolls were also referred to as "rolls," and it is possible that the term "roles" came from this usage.

How to Make Your Own Scrolls

One can make up one's own scrolls for parts with an electronic version of the text.

The materials needed are quite readily available except for the dowels which form their basis. I have seen people make scrolls of unsharpened pencils, but those are too short and thin for an effective scroll base. You need two ½-inch dowels 8–9-inches long, paper, scissors, scotch tape, and covered hair elastics. (Dowel rods come in varying lengths; you can get several scrolls from one rod.)

Of course, once you make a digital cue script you can read it on your phone or mobile device. However, I find that having a physical scroll leads to quicker memorization.

Starting with the digital file for the script, using Word or similar software, just cut out everyone else's lines except for their cues for your character's lines. A cue wouldn't be the full prior speech but just the last 3–5 words of their speech.

The text should be formatted so that it is in a large enough font to be easily readable and formatted so that it is no wider than 5-inches wide.

Print out your scroll, trim the paper so that it is about 6–6½ inches wide, and tape it to one of the dowels. As you trim the pages, tape them together so that they flow continuously. While you add to your role you can roll what you have done on to the dowel and secure it with a binder clip to keep it from unrolling. When you get to the end of the end of your role, you tape it to the other dowel.

Then you use the hair rubber bands to hold the dowels together and move back and forth in the part. As you become comfortable you can easily advance the scroll with one hand.

ADVICE TO ACTORS

John Russell Brown

There is no such person as a "Shakespearean actor," if that phrase implies the possession of unique qualifications or unusual gifts. Shakespeare's plays are available to all good actors, no matter what their training or experience may be.

Yet, of course, the texts reprinted here are not like those of modern plays. Shakespeare does present special problems, and the blunt assurance that his writing is open for anyone to explore will not sound very convincing to a student-actor meeting it for the first time. The following approaches are offered as encouragement to make a start and free imagination to work intelligently on the texts.

Character

First of all, an actor in any play must discover the person behind the words of any particular role. Of course, an actor must learn how to speak the character's lines clearly and forcefully, but that alone will not bring the play to life. Speech is not all, because Shakespeare did not write for talking heads. He first imagined individual persons in lively interplay with each other and *then* conjured words for them to speak; and that is the best sequence for an actor to follow. A living person has to be brought to the stage, and then he can begin to speak and become realized in the process.

In Elizabethan times, plays were performed on a large platform stage that jutted out into the middle of a crowded audience, many of whom were standing rather than sitting as is the custom today; and in this open arena everything took place by daylight. Some performances were given indoors, but then the audience was illuminated along with the actors. Such conditions were more like those of a public meeting in our day, or of a booth in a fairground. They called for an acting style that was grounded in a basic physical delineation of each character. An actor had to maintain the vibrant outlines of the role so that his performance could be viewed from all sides and at all times whenever he was on stage.

Character Questions

BASIC QUESTIONS:

- How does the character move and speak?
- How think and feel?
- Where does this individual come from? What does he know? What does he want?
- What does he look like, sound like?
- How could anyone recognize the person who speaks these lines?
- Why does this particular person need to speak these particular words?
- How old is this person?
- What physical characteristics are essential for an impersonation?
- What is this person's family situation?
- What are the political, professional, and social conditions of his life?

MORE DIFFICULT QUESTIONS FOLLOW, WHICH HELP TO DEFINE PERSONALITY AND CONSCIOUSNESS:

- How does this person "see" and respond to the world around him?
- What does he like and dislike? What does he pursue and what does he seek to avoid?
- What conventions, social pressures, or political forces influence behavior, either consciously or unconsciously?

INTERROGATING THE TEXT:

- What verbs does the character use?
- How does he talk to other characters?
- Do questions, assertions, explanations, answers, excuses, qualifications, elaborations, or repetitions predominate?
- Are sentences long or short, leisured and assured, or compact and urgent?
- Are sentences governed by a single main verb?

- Or are they supplied with a sequence of phrases, each governed by its own subsidiary verb?
- How does this person refer to others: always in the same way, or with variations? With different names, titles, or endearments?
- Is address intimate or formal, simple or elaborate?
- Or is contact between two characters assumed and assured, so that names are not required at all?

Normally such detailed verbal enquiry is a continuous process that goes on throughout a long rehearsal period. Scrutiny of every word in even a short scene will help to develop a sensitivity to words, a facility that can be drawn upon constantly throughout an actor's career in whatever plays he may perform.

ALL KINDS OF EXERCISES CAN HELP:
- Very slow rehearsals encourage full awareness of what is thought and felt, as the words are spoken easily without thought of projecting or shaping them.
- Silent rehearsals, with someone else speaking the text.
- Improvised explorations of moments of encounter or retreat.
- Improvised paraphrasing of Shakespeare's text.
- Sessions in which the actors sit back-to-back and only speak the words, trying to communicate fully.
- Variations in positions, so that the two actors are at first close and then far apart, quite still and then always on the move, looking at each other or refusing to do so, paying attention to nothing but the sound of words or engaged on other business—all these explorations may find new means of expression or more physical enactments for a scene.
- Questions should be asked, as for any play, to encourage a fuller sense of what is afoot in a scene: What do they expect from each other? How secure or insecure are they?

What we can deduce about Elizabethan stage practice should encourage present-day actors to seek out distinctive physical characteristics for each role they play in Shakespeare, possess or embody them as fully as possible, and then play the text boldly. This will provide the appropriate dynamic and credibility.

The moment actors walk onto the stage in character, they must be strong and expressive, even before a word has been spoken. Then as each person is drawn into the drama, there must be no loss of definition but growth, development, and surprise. As the play continues, new facets and new resources will be revealed, until each character has become fully present and open to an audience. In performance, actors need to be alert and active and must possess great reserves of energy. They are like boxers in a ring who dare not lose concentration or the ability to perform at full power. They have to watch, listen, move, and speak, and at the same time embody the persons they represent. It is like levitating, or flying through the air, by a continuous act of will and imagination. Characters must have clarity; actors, courage.

But how can an actor find the person to present? Trial and error play no small role in shaping a trained instinct for Shakespeare's people. And this trial begins with a close interrogation of the text.

In a search for the person to bring onstage, first impressions may be deceptive or, rather, limiting. For example, on a first reading, Romeo and Juliet may appear to be two "typical" romantic lovers who delight in each other's presence and have much in common, including parents who would disapprove very strongly of their love if they were to know of it. All that is true and useful, but if the two actors for these roles were each to make a list of the nouns in their respective speeches, two very different sensibilities and personalities would be revealed. The minds of Romeo and Juliet run in different directions; they have their own sensations and feelings, and distinct views of the world around them.

There are many constructive ways of studying Shakespeare's words beyond tracing verb patterns. Preparing lists of adjectives and adverbs may reveal when and where a character is sufficiently thoughtful to qualify an idea, although some speakers in some scenes will never have sufficient command or perception to use a qualifying or descriptive word. Lists of double meanings, similes, metaphors, references to other realities than the one on-stage—whether the imagined world is distant, intimate, literary, political, religious, or historical—can help to show the deeper resources of a character's mind.

Slowly, by such analysis of the text, a psychological "identikit" can be assembled, marking predominant colors, preconceptions, modes of thought and feeling. Many such separate and small details begin to suggest a more embracing idea about a person.

On the other hand, it would be a mistake to read and analyze for too long; an actor needs to start to act and to speak just as soon as intuition and imagination are quickened by more deliberate investigations. The actor's own being has to be satisfied and used in performance, as well as the details of the text.

Slowly, a sense of the character's consciousness will emerge, and a number of physical traits will become established. So, the stage character should evolve slowly, from within itself, freshly and uniquely created; actions will suit the words and reveal a sense of being that attracts and repays attention. There is no knowing what may happen. One danger is that too many details will attract attention so that the basic presence is left undeveloped. After making his discoveries, the actor must therefore decide which of his discoveries are truly necessary and which can be discarded.

Careful and patient study, analysis, exploration, imitation, quiet impulse, quick imagination, and the luck of adventurous rehearsal all have a contribution to make in the creation of these plays.

Verse, Prose, and Language

Laurence Olivier in his portrayal of the lead in *Henry the Fifth* decided to be real, rather than phony, grand, or rhetorical. So he "got underneath the lines," and in rehearsal his acting became so close to natural behavior that the words were sometimes indistinct and difficult to hear. Then one day, Tyrone Guthrie, the director, stopped the rehearsal—he had been away for a while and insisted that this actor should perform the verse and the rhetoric: "Larry . . . let's have it properly," he called out from the back of the theater. For a moment, Olivier hesitated and then did as he was told; and the change, as he tells the story, was instantaneous and transforming. He had always known that verse and sentence structure, and imagery, were instructing him to speak with confidence, enjoyment, and resonance, and that they had a commanding and developing power, but he had held back in distrust. Now he found that artificial verse and grand language fitted his character like necessary and proper clothes, and they gave him the ability to rouse his audience on stage and in the auditorium. (When he came to act the part in the film, they even roused his horse.) Olivier was still truthful, but now he was also heroic.

Poetry is the natural idiom of Shakespeare's stage, as swimming is for the ocean, singing for opera or musical theater, controlled and exceptional movement for dance, or solemnity for great occasions. Speaking Shakespeare's verse becomes as instinctive as song, and the actor forgets that he is being metrically correct and vocally subtle.

Elizabethan audiences were so convinced by performances in which verse was spoken that a play written wholly in prose would be more likely to seem artificial. Today Shakespeare's plays can become *just* as real, if actors both use the verse and also act with truth to life. Bernard Shaw advised actors in Shakespeare's early plays to treat the verse like a child does a swing, without self-consciousness or hesitation. In later plays the art of verse is more demanding and the pleasure it gives deeper, but both must be similarly instinctive.

Until verse speaking has become second nature—as it quite quickly does—an actor should study the meter of the lines well in advance of rehearsals, methodically picking out the words to be stressed and finding, by trial and error, the most appropriate phrasing. It is necessary to speak the lines out loud, so that meaning and syntax can be related to the demands of versification and *vice versa*. Breathing and speaking should work together so that the energy of thought and feeling responds to the text and begins to motivate speech. Texture, linked variations of sound, alliteration, assonance, rhyme, and rhythm must all be heeded. These concepts cannot be explored fully in the mind. By speaking the words, their sounds and visceral impact will reveal different levels of meaning. Phrasing, breathing, tempo, pace, pitch, intonation, silence have all to be considered. The lines must be spoken aloud again and again, as one way of speaking is tested against another; and then, slowly, by following the clues inherent in the text, a fully responsive delivery can emerge.

When using this book, start to "do" whenever doubt arises. Generations of actors will assure you that with practice, the acting of Shakespeare's poetry—not merely the speaking of it—becomes instinctive and fluent, pleasurable and, in the context of the play, both true and natural.

The actor should begin by appreciating Shakespeare's preferred medium, the iambic pentameter. Each line should have ten syllables, alternately weak and strong, so that each pair of syllables forms one "foot," and five feet complete a line. Although few pentameters are entirely regular—

if they were, the dialogue would be unbearably wooden and predictable—all follow the ongoing pattern to some degree. It is their likeness that links them together, while their irregularity draws attention to particular words, varies rhythm and pace, and lends a forward movement to speech as disturbance of pattern awakens an expectation that pattern will be reasserted and finally satisfied.

STEPS TO ANALYZING THE TEXT

- Is it verse or prose?
- If verse, is it regular or irregular? Many lines are irregular with stresses not following the iambic pattern or if there are other than ten syllables in a line.
- Speak the text to find the most natural emphasis.

Sense, syntax, speakability, and an underlying regularity are the principal guides in scanning a line, but they do not always provide an unequivocal lead. Until well-practiced in verse speaking, a student should mark the text in pencil, changing the stresses until sure enough to start rehearsals. Still more changes may be made later, before this slow and methodical preparation can be forgotten and taken for granted—that is the last and absolutely necessary part of the process.

Scansion

In deciding how to scan a line, some general rules may be applied. Nouns and verbs always need to be stressed in order to make the sense clear—more stressed than adjectives, adverbs, pronouns, prepositions, or conjunctions. Moreover the fourth syllable of any line, being the most able to reestablish the normal pattern after irregularities and most in control of each individual line, is nearly always stressed in a regular way. If the end of a line is irregular, the beginning of the following one is likely to be regular, for two, or three, consecutive feet. However, the first foot in a line is very frequently irregular, since a reversed foot, with the strong syllable coming first, gives fresh impetus to new thought.

An example from an early play gives clear indication of both regularity and irregularity:

(King Edward speaks to his queen about political enemies.)

My love, forbear to fawn upon their frowns.

What danger or what sorrow can befall thee

So long as Edward is thy constant friend

And their true sovereign whom they must obey?

Nay, whom they shall obey, and love thee too,   5

Unless they seek for hatred at my hands-

Which if they do, yet will I keep thee safe

And they shall feel the vengeance of my wrath.
(*Henry VI, Part iii*, IV.i.75–82)

Some of the strong stresses marked in these lines might be changed, but very few; and all its irregularities are brief. The close of line 5 is most problematical: it is marked here with three consecutive strong syllables as the sense of the parenthesis seems to require, but the final "too" might be unstressed or, possibly, the penultimate "thee." (Three consecutive strong stresses should be used very sparingly, because they doubly disturb the underlying norm.) A similar uncertainty arises at the end of line 2, which is marked here with the final "thee" as an extra unstressed syllable. Alternatively, "can" would not be stressed and "befall" counted as a single strong syllable, so that "thee" could follow with equal stress.

All the strong syllables are not equally stressed in speech, and here actors have much more liberty to find the emphasis that suits their own interpretation of a character. Many choices are available. In most iambic pentameters only three syllables take major emphasis, the other stressed syllables being only slightly more prominent than the unstressed ones. So one reading of the same passage might be:

My love, *forbear* to *fawn* upon their *frowns.*
What *danger* or what sorrow can *befall* thee

> So *long* as Edward is thy constant friend
> And their true sovereign whom they *must obey?*
> Nay, whom they *shall* obey, and *love thee* too,
> Unless they *seek* for *hatred* at my *hands*
> Which if they *do,* yet will I *keep* thee *safe*
> And they shall feel the *vengeance* of my *wrath.*

Perhaps the first line should have four major emphases, as Edward presses his argument. In line 3, "constant" may be more significant than "long" and so take the emphasis; but the "f" in *friend* makes that word able to gain strength from the other stressed *f*s in the preceding lines. Choice of stress will also be influenced by words set either in opposition to contrast with each other or in agreement to reinforce each other. Stressing these words can often clarify the logic of what the speaker is saying. For example, in line 4, "their" might be stressed and the penultimate foot reversed, so that "they" is stressed as well for reinforcement, and "must" would count only as a weak syllable. Such a reading would raise the possibility that in line 7, "thee" might be stressed rather than "keep," so that the "they" in line 8 could be a fourth major emphasis in contrast with "thee," to bring a relatively sturdy finish to the whole speech. But, in general, pronouns should not be emphasized, because that takes away prominence from the nouns and verbs, which have to sustain the sense of any speech; those are the elements that form the supporting backbone for strong dialogue and provide its thought-action and forward impetus.

This simple speech of eight lines illustrates how metrical considerations become, very quickly and necessarily, issues of character as well. The same is true when problems of phrasing are introduced. In the early verse plays especially, a brief pause at the end of each line is usual and provides a further guide to phrasing beyond those inherent in sense and syntax. Yet this is not a constant rule, and sometimes only the slightest rise of pitch or marking of a final consonant is sufficient indication of a line-ending; in this way, two consecutive lines will run into each other almost without hesitation or change of impression. In this passage, if Edward pauses slightly after "friend," the last word of line 3, and after "safe" at the end of line 8, his thoughts of "love" will seem more urgent than those concerning political power because, in this reading, the latter will seem to be afterthoughts. But if line 3 runs over into line 4, without the customary pause at the line-ending, the two reactions become almost inseparable; and then the political motivation will outweigh the amorous, because it is expressed in a longer phrase and placed in a climactic position. The relationship between lines 7 and 8 raises similar possibilities.

A pause, or caesura, may also be marked in mid-line. Syntax or sense will sometimes require this to be done (as in line 7 above), but here too a choice is often to be made. The advantage of a mid-line break is that it can give a sense of ongoing thought and quick intelligence. Some critics would argue that every line should have its caesura, but there is good reason not to supply them too strongly or too consistently; such readings encourage a halting delivery and an impression of weakness, and are not always easy to comprehend. In this passage, the final line would clearly be stronger if there were no hint of a pause in mid-line. So might line 2—unless two slight pauses were given, as if commas had been placed after both "danger" and "sorrow," thus giving Edward a very thoughtful and determined manner of speech. Line 6 also seems to run without a break, unless it came after "seek," so giving point to Edward's personal involvement. Seldom should a mid-line pause be placed so that it breaks up a regular iambic foot; normally it should follow, and therefore still further emphasize, a strong syllable. If a caesura is marked in each line of this passage, a general impression of energetic thought might be given, and in some performances this could be useful.

No decision is solely a technical matter; versification in Shakespeare's mind was an instrument for enhancing a representation of individual characters in lively interplay. Problems of verse-speaking are truly dramatic problems, and so each actor must find solutions that suit his or her own impersonation. Although there are many ways of speaking verse that are clearly wrong—too many stressed syllables one after another is a common fault, and too few clear stresses another—there is no one correct way to speak any speech. A respect for versification offers many opportunities to strengthen one's grasp of the play in action and deepen the rendering of a character's very being.

As in any lifelike dialogue in prose, the actor must ask why speak at all; that is, he must discover and follow the action of thought and feeling beneath the words, sustaining and shaping them. In other terms, syntax is, in the last analysis, more important than meter. Each complete sentence is a distinct action, requiring breath, physical response, and speech, according to its own impulses.

In prose dialogue, sentence structure is the principal means whereby Shakespeare controls and so strengthens an actor's speaking of his text. Often the formal arrangement is very elaborate and sustained. Moreover, its effect is reinforced by the use of a series of parallel phrases and by wordplay; these both hold the subsections together and provide a sense of growth and climax. Exploring how the words play off each other in these ways can reveal the character's intentions. Stressing key words, puns, and affirmations is not enough; the flow and energy of the language have to be represented in performance, giving a sense of exploration, energy, struggle, attainment, frustration. Sentence structure and wordplay define this music and this drama, and the actor must respond to both and transmit both through performance.

Each actor must make his own distinctive response to the challenge of the text. No teacher or director can provide ready-made and sufficient solutions here, and this realization may help to understand something fundamental about the acting of Shakespeare: no instruction can take responsibility away from the actors. Sometimes students are recommended to speak Shakespeare's lines with a certain quality or tone of voice, or a certain accent, and for some exercises or some productions this may be useful. But following such a prescription is likely to do more harm than good, because the actor is distracted from the primary task of finding a voice and being for each character and then responding to the text in his or her own manner. Of course, efficient breathing and voice production are needed to respond to so demanding a text, but technical expertise must always be at the service of the specific demands of character, situation, and speech, as these are discovered by each individual actor.

Some words and phrases in the plays seem to cry out for a great deal of preparatory work, but it may be only a small exaggeration to say that every word, phrase, sentence, and speech may repay in some measure a similar investment. An actor can have an endless adventure when acting Shakespeare, as step by step he gets closer to a fully responsive, individual, and necessary (and therefore convincing) way of turning text into performance.

An actor's mind and body need to be more than usually alert and energized to answer the challenge. What starts as patient and complicated exploration can end, however, in a marvelous extension of an actor's powers of thought, feeling, and being, as the poetry comes to fresh and brilliant life. That is why Shakespeare's plays are so rewarding to perform. By making each word sound as if it is necessary to his or her character, an actor will claim attention with amazing ease.

Toward Performance

All kinds of exercises can help inexperienced actors. Very slow rehearsals encourage full awareness of what is thought and felt, as the words are spoken easily without thought of projecting or shaping them. Silent rehearsals, with someone else speaking the text, improvised explorations of moments of encounter or retreat, improvised paraphrasing of Shakespeare's text, or sessions in which the actors sit back-to-back and only speak the words, trying to communicate fully—all these devices may help performers to become more free, adventurous, and true. Variations in positions, so that the two actors are at first close and then far apart, quite still and then always on the move, looking at each other or refusing to do so, paying attention to nothing but the sound of words or engaged on other business—all these explorations may find new means of expression or more physical enactments for a scene. Questions should be asked, as for any play, to encourage a fuller sense of what is afoot in a scene: What do they expect from each other? How secure or insecure are they? Many of these questions were first asked in individual preparation. None of these ordinary ways of working is foreign to Shakespeare's plays.

When performing modern plays, actors have extensive stage directions in the text to guide them: descriptions of activity, unspoken reactions, movements, pauses, silences, and so on. But in Shakespeare's plays there is little of this, and what is printed in modern editions is often the invention of editors and not what Shakespeare wrote. In the versions of scenes printed in this book, stage directions are very scarce and minimal, but the commentary will often point out activity, movement and responses, that *may* be required for acting the text.

Actors must learn to read Shakespeare's stage directions implicit in the dialogue: clues for tempo, rhythm change, breathing, for closeness or distance between the characters, and so on. Very important, because usually unambiguous, is Shakespeare's use of incomplete verse lines to indicate a pause or silence in the middle of speech, or in the interchange between two people. When two characters share a single verse line, each speaking one half of a regular iambic pentameter, the opposite is true; there should be no pause or hesitation here, the dialogue continuing without break and the new speaker responsive to the phrasing, rhythm, and pitch of the person he follows.

So much can be discovered while working together on a text that simplification must become part of the ongoing process. Actors must identify those elements that are truest and most revealing and develop those at the cost of losing others. The essential part of this process is to recognize what is particularly alive and new in the work and take the necessary steps to allow this to grow.

There is a paradox at the heart of what can be said about the task of acting Shakespeare's plays. Imaginatively the performers need to be exceptionally free, and yet the most liberating work will be found by paying strict attention to the minutest details of the text and using them as spurs to invention and exploration. Shakespeare's imagination seems always to be ahead of ours, beckoning us; and so, if the actor is patient and adventurous, he will find within the text whatever suits his or her individual abilities and point of view. The text can be ever new, and even the most experienced actor or playgoer is liable to be amazed at what is achieved for the first time with any new production.

Of course, actors develop particular ways of working, and their interpretations of a number of roles will have much in common, but it is wise to beware of drawing the possibilities of a Shakespeare text down to the level of performance that a particular actor has found to be reliable. Shakespeare's kings are all different from each other, and so are his fools; and each one is liable to have a different life from scene to scene, sometimes even moment by moment. Even such clear distinctions as that between comedy and drama should be treated with reserve: in important ways, there are no comic and no serious roles in Shakespeare. Hamlet or Prince Hal, Romeo or Juliet all need to raise laughter and act the fool, drawing on skills that are sometimes considered to be appropriate to comedy. Lady Macbeth and Macbeth are deeply involved in a terrible action, but their minds move with swiftness and fantasy, so they play with words, very like witty persons in a comedy. In all Shakespeare's roles, villain or hero, lover or fool, an actor must be ready to respond outside conventional limitations.

When Shakespeare's Prince Hamlet tried to instruct the players who arrived in the court of Elsinore, he was concerned with their technique and their attention to the text, but "their special observance," he said, should be with "nature":

> for anything so o'erdone is from the purpose of playing, whose end, both at the first and now, was and is to hold, as 'twere, the mirror up to nature....
>
> *(Hamlet*, III.ii.1 ff.)

The key phrase, "hold the mirror up to nature," sounds like a generalized instruction: show everyone what they look like, but in context it is precise. Hamlet is in the process of castigating actors' faults and he continues in the same vein:

> O there be players that I have seen play—and heard others praise, and that highly—not to speak it profanely, that, neither having th'accent of Christians, nor the gait of Christian, pagan nor man, have so strutted and bellowed that I have thought some of Nature's journeymen had made men, and not made them well, they imitated humanity so abominably.

The actors have to "make men"; they have to be highly skilled craftspersons, not ordinary workmen ("journeymen"). Characters have to move and speak, and function, as we do: they have been individually crafted and must be alive with individuality. Slowly, skillfully, and adventurously, an actor must build an illusion of a living being, one for whom Shakespeare's text is a necessary extension of existence. Hamlet does not speak for Shakespeare, but in creating this character the dramatist wrote with such freedom, precision, and obvious pleasure that he must have drawn more deeply than usual on his own ideas and reactions. Lacking Shakespeare's advice to the players, Hamlet's is a good substitute.

Another Perspective

Neil Freeman

For another perspective on this famous speech, here is Neil Freeman's Folio version of the text with his commentary:

Speake the Speech I pray you, as I pronounc'd   3.2.1–45

Background: Just before the playing of the requested "The Murther of Gonzago" (with "some dosen or sixteene lines" added by Hamlet for Claudius's benefit), Hamlet seems to feel the need to instruct the actors in their business (or as the scholars suggest, Shakespeare felt the need to remind *his* own actors of *their* craft, which some of them seem to have neglected).

Style: general address to a small group
Where: somewhere near the great hall of the castle
To Whom: the first player and colleagues (an unspecified number)
# of Lines: 40   **Probable Timing:** 2.00 minutes

Hamlet 1   Speake the Speech I pray you, as I pronounc'd
it to you trippingly on the Tongue : But if you mouth it,
as many of your Players do, I had as live the Town-Cryer
had spoke my Lines : Nor do not saw the Ayre too much [ ]
your hand thus, but use all gently ; for in the verie Torrent,
Tempest, and (as I may say) the Whirle-winde of [ ]
Passion, you must acquire and beget a Temperance that
may give it Smoothnesse .

2   O it offends mee to the Soule, to
[see] a robustious Pery-wig-pated Fellow teare a Passion to tatters, to verie ragges, to split the eares of the
Groundlings : who (for the most part) are capeable of
nothing, but inexplicable dumbe shewes, & noise : I [could]
have such a Fellow whipt for o're-doing Termagant : it
out-Herod's Herod .

3   Pray you avoid it .

---

4   Be not too tame neyther : but let your owne
Discretion be your Tutor .

5   Sute the Action to the Word,
the Word to the Action, with this speciall observance : That
you [ore-stop] not the modestie of Nature ; for any
thing so [over-done], is [frö] the purpose of Playing, whose
end both at the first and now, was and is, to hold as 'twer

the Mirrour up to Nature ;   to shew Vertue her owne
Feature, Scorne her owne Image, and the verie Age and
Bodie of the Time, his forme and pressure .

6   Now, this
over-done, or come tardie off, though it [make] the unskil-
full laugh, cannot but make the Judicious greeve ; The
censure of the which One, must in your allowance o're-
way a whole Theater of Others .

7   Oh, there bee Players that
I have seene Play, and heard others praise, and that highly
(not to speake it prophanely) that neyther having the accent
of Christians, nor the [gate] of Christian, Pagan, [or Norman],
have so strutted and bellowed, that I have thought some
of Natures Jouerney-men had made men, and not made
them well, they imitated Humanity so abhominably .

---

8   And let those that
play your Clownes, speake no more [then] is set downe for
them .

9   For there be of them, that will themselves laugh,
to set on some quantitie of barren Spectators to laugh
too, though in the meane time, some necessary Question
of the Play be [then] to be considered : that's Villanous, &
shewes a most pittifull Ambition in the Foole that uses it .

10 Go make you readie .

The speech is essentially composed of two parts, Hamlet's instructions to the actors and his seemingly irrelevant digressions into his own reflections upon and reactions to what he regards as "bad acting"—and although commentators offer several contemporary explanations as to why, to satisfy an audience, there still must be a theatrical reason to justify these distractions. F's orthography shows that whereas the instructions are mainly intellectual, the sidebars are either emotional or passionate—the need to release seeming to be very important, perhaps suggesting his distress with all the bad real-life acting going on around him (Claudius, Rosincrance, Guildensterne, and even Ophelia).

- The importance of the forthcoming event is underscored by there being virtually no unembellished lines throughout the forty-one lines of advice and reminiscence until the very last words, F #10's "Go make you readie."

- The short F #3, "Pray you avoid it," is the other interesting exception, for both it and the very few surround phrases seem to go beyond just advice to the players, but reveal Hamlet's need for outward signs of honorable behavior from all around him:

> . Nor do not saw the Ayre too much [ ] your hand thus, but
>   use all gently ;
> : I could have such a Fellow whipt for o're-doing Termagant :
>   it out-Herod's Herod .
> : that's Villanous, & shewes a most pittifull Ambition in the
>   Foole that uses it .

- The opening advice of "Speake the Speech" is strongly intellectual (F #1, 15/6), only to be broken by strong emotion as he becomes sidetracked into expressing at length what "offends mee to the Soule" (5/9, F #2's first four and a half lines), while the thought of whipping the "Fellow" who offends him becomes totally intellectual (4/0 in F #2's last two surround phrase line and a half)

- After the quiet imploring of the short F #3, as Hamlet returns to his series of instructions his passions return (F #4, 2/2), which he quickly reins in, reestablishing intellectual control (21/9, F #5–6) for the remainder of his instructions

- But once more, as he breaks off into describing bad actors whose performances have offended him, his intellect gives way, this time to passion (8/9, F #7)

- Commentators acknowledge that F #8–9 is a contemporary reference to the "Clownes" of his own company improvising too much, so it's hardly surprising that this moment is first emotional (1/3, F #8), then with the intellectual elaboration (3/1, F #9's first three and a half lines), quickly turning to passion in his final surround phrase denunciation (3/3, F #9's last line and half)

- And after all the verbiage and sidetracks, as the time grows near for the performance that Hamlet hopes will reveal all, at last Hamlet becomes quiet (the unembellished F #10)

BRIEF BACKGROUND TO THE FIRST FOLIO

Neil Freeman

The First Folio

The end of 1623 saw the publication of the justifiably famed First Folio (F1). The single volume, published in a run of approximately one thousand copies at the princely sum of one pound (a tremendous risk, considering that a single play would sell at no more than six pence, one-fortieth of F1's price, and that the annual salary of a schoolmaster was only ten pounds), contained thirty-six plays.

The manuscripts from which each F1 play would be printed came from a variety of sources. Some had already been printed. Some came from the playhouse complete with production details. Some had no theatrical input at all but were handsomely copied out and easy to read. Some were supposedly very messy, complete with first draft scribbles and crossings out. Yet, as Charlton Hinman, the revered dean of First Folio studies, describes F1 in the Introduction to the Norton Facsimile:

> It is of inestimable value for what it is, for what it contains. For here are preserved the masterworks of the man universally recognized as our greatest writer; and preserved, as Ben Jonson realized at the time of the original publication, not for an age but for all time.

What Does F1 Represent?

- texts prepared for actors who rehearsed three days for a new play and one day for one already in the repertoire
- written in a style (rhetoric incorporating debate) so different from ours (grammatical) that many modern alterations based on grammar (or poetry) have done remarkable harm to the rhetorical/debate quality of the original text and thus to interpretations of characters
- written for an acting company the core of which steadily grew older, and whose skills and interests changed markedly over twenty years as well as for an audience whose makeup and interests likewise changed as the company grew more experienced

The whole is based upon supposedly the best documents available at the time, collected by men closest to Shakespeare throughout his career, and brought to a single printing house whose errors are now widely understood—far more than those of some of the printing houses that produced the original quartos.

The Key Question

What text have you been working with—a good modern text or an "original" text, that is, a copy of one of the first printings of the play?

If it's a modern text, no matter how well edited, despite all the learned information offered, it's not surprising that you feel somewhat at a loss, for there is a huge difference between the original printings (the First Folio and the individual quartos) and any text prepared after 1700 right up to the most modern of editions. All the post-1700 texts have been tidied up for the modern reader to ingest silently, revamped according to the rules of correct grammar, syntax, and poetry. However, the "originals" were prepared for actors speaking aloud, playing characters often in a great deal of emotional and/or intellectual stress, and were set down on paper according to the very flexible rules of rhetoric and a seemingly very cavalier attitude toward the rules of grammar, and syntax, and spelling, and capitalization, and even poetry.

Unfortunately, because of the grammatical and syntactical standardization in place by the early 1700s, many of the quirks and oddities of the original also have been dismissed as "accidental"—usually as compositor error either in deciphering the original manuscript, falling prey to their own particular idiosyncrasies, or not having calculated correctly the amount of space needed to set the text. Modern texts dismiss the possibility that these very quirks and oddities may be by Shakespeare, hearing his characters in as much difficulty as poor Peter Quince is in *A Midsummer Night's Dream* (when he, as the Prologue, terrified and struck down by stage fright, makes a huge grammatical hash in introducing his play "Pyramus and Thisbe" before the aristocracy, whose acceptance or rejection can make or break him):

> If we offend, it is with our good will.
> That you should think, we come not to offend,
> But with good will.

>   To show our simple skill,
> That is the true beginning of our end .
> Consider then, we come but in despite.
> We do not come, as minding to content you ,
> Our true intent is.
>   All for your delight
> We are not here.
>   That you should here repent you,
> The Actors are at hand; and by their show,
> You shall know all, that you are like to know.
>
>   (*A Midsummer Night's Dream*)

In many other cases in the complete works what was originally printed is equally "peculiar," but, unlike Peter Quince, these peculiarities are usually regularized by most modern texts.

Most of these "peculiarities" resulted from Shakespeare setting down for his actors the stresses, trials, and tribulations the characters are experiencing as they think and speak, and thus are theatrical gold dust for the actor, director, scholar, teacher, and general reader alike.

The First Essential Difference between the Two Texts: Thinking

A **modern** text can show:

- the story line
- your character's conflict with the world at large
- your character's conflict with certain individuals within that world

but because of the very way an "original" text was set, it can show you all this plus one key extra, the very thing that makes big speeches what they are:

- the conflict within the character

Why?

Any good playwright writes about characters in stressful situations who are often in a state of conflict, not only with the world around them and the people in that world, but also within themselves. And you probably know from personal experience that when these conflicts occur, people do not necessarily utter the most perfect of grammatical/poetic/syntactic statements, phrases, or sentences. Joy and delight, pain and sorrow often come sweeping through in the way things are said, in the incoherence of the phrases, the running together of normally disassociated ideas, and even in the sounds of the words themselves.

The tremendous advantage of the period in which Shakespeare was setting his plays down on paper and how they first appeared in print was that when characters were rational and in control of self and situation, their phrasing and sentences (and poetic structure) would appear to be quite normal even to a modern eye—but when things were going wrong, these sentences and phrasing (and poetic structure) would become highly erratic. But the Quince-type eccentricities are rarely allowed to stand. Sadly, in tidying, most modern texts usually make the text far too clean, thus setting rationality when none originally existed.

The Second Essential Difference between First Folio and Modern Texts: Speaking, Arguing, Debating

Having discovered what and how you or your character is thinking is only the first stage of the work. You/the character then have to speak aloud, in a society that absolutely loved to speak—and not only speak ideas (content) but to speak entertainingly so as to keep listeners enthralled (and this was especially so when you have little content to offer and have to mask it somehow; think of today's television adverts and political spin doctors as a parallel, and you get the picture). Indeed one of the Elizabethan "how to win an argument" books was very precise about this: George Puttenham, *The Art of English Poesie* (1589).

Elizabethan Schooling

All educated classes could debate/argue at the drop of a hat, for both boys (in "petty-schools") and girls (by books and tutors) were trained in what was known overall as the art of rhetoric, which itself was split into three parts:

- First, how to distinguish the real from false appearances/outward show (think of the three caskets in *The Merchant of Venice* in which the lan-

guage on the gold and silver caskets enticingly, and deceptively, seems to offer hopes of great personal rewards that are dashed when the language is carefully explored, whereas once the apparent threat on the lead casket is carefully analyzed, the reward therein is the greatest that could be hoped for).
- Second, how to frame your argument on one of "three great grounds": honor/morality; justice/legality; and, when all else fails, expedience/practicality.
- Third, how to order and phrase your argument so winsomely that your audience will vote for you no matter how good the opposition—and there were well over two hundred rules and variations by which winning could be achieved, all of which had to be assimilated before a child's education was considered over and done with.

THINKING ON YOUR FEET: THAT IS, THE QUICK, DEFT, RAPID MODIFICATION OF EACH TINY THOUGHT

The Elizabethan—therefore, your character, and therefore, you—was also trained to explore and modify thoughts as they spoke—never would you see a sentence in its entirety and have it perfectly worked out in your mind before you spoke (unless it was a deliberately written, formal public declaration, as with the Officer of the Court in *The Winter's Tale*, reading the charges against Hermione). Thus, after uttering your very first phrase, you might expand it, or modify it, deny it, change it, and so on throughout the whole sentence and speech.

From the poet Samuel Taylor Coleridge, there is a wonderful description of how Shakespeare put thoughts together like "a serpent twisting and untwisting in its own strength," that is, with one thought springing out of the one previous. Treat each new phrase as a fresh unraveling of the serpent's coil. What is discovered (and therefore said) is only revealed as the old coil/phrase disappears, revealing a new coil in its place. The new coil is the new thought. The old coil moves/disappears because the previous phrase is finished with as soon as it is spoken.

MODERN APPLICATION

It is very rarely that we speak dispassionately in our "real" lives. After all, thoughts give rise to feelings, feelings give rise to thoughts, and we usually speak both together—unless

1. we're trying very hard for some reason to control ourselves and not give ourselves away;

2. or the volcano of emotions within us is so strong that we cannot control ourselves, and feelings swamp thoughts;

3. and sometimes whether deliberately or unconsciously, we color words according to our feelings; the humanity behind the words so revealed is instantly understandable.

How the Original Texts Naturally Enhance/Underscore This Control or Release

The amazing thing about the way all Elizabethan/early Jacobean texts were first set down (the term used to describe the printed words on the page being "orthography"), is that it was flexible, allowing for such variations to be automatically set down without fear of grammatical repercussion.

So if Shakespeare heard Juliet's Nurse working hard to try to convince Juliet that the Prince's nephew Juliet is being forced to (bigamously) marry, instead of setting the everyday normal

> O he's a lovely gentleman

which the modern texts HAVE to set, the first printings were permitted to set

> O hee's a Lovely Gentleman

suggesting that something might be going on inside the Nurse that causes her to release such excessive energy.

Be Careful

This needs to be stressed very carefully: the orthography doesn't dictate to you/force you to accept exactly what it means. The orthography simply suggests that you might want to explore this moment further or more deeply.

In other words, simply because of the flexibility with which the Elizabethans/Shakespeare could set down on paper what they heard in their minds or wanted their listeners to hear, in addition to all the modern acting necessities of character—situation, objective, intention, action, and tactics—the original Shakespeare texts offer pointers to where feelings (either emotional or intellectual, or when combined together as passion, both) are also evident.

Summary

Basic Approach to First Folio Speeches on the Following Pages:

1. First, use the modern version shown first. By doing so you can discover:

- the basic plot line of what's happening to the character
- the first set of conflicts/obstacles impinging on the character as a result of the situation or actions of other characters
- the supposed grammatical and poetical correctness of the speech

2. Then you can explore:

- any acting techniques you'd apply to any modern soliloquy, including establishing for the character
- the given circumstances of the scene
- their outward state of being (who they are sociologically, etc.)
- their intentions and objectives
- the resultant action and tactics they decide to pursue

3. When this is complete, consult the First Folio version of the text. This will help you discover and explore:

- the precise thinking and debating process so essential to an understanding of any Shakespeare text
- the moments when the text is *not* grammatically or poetically as correct as the modern texts would have you believe, which will in turn help you recognize the moments of conflict and struggle stemming from within the character itself
- the sense of fun and enjoyment Shakespeare's language nearly always offers you no matter how dire the situation

Should you wish to further explore even more the differences between the two texts, the commentary that follows discusses how the First Folio has been changed and what those alterations might mean for the human arc of the speech.

Notes on How the First Folio Speeches Are Set Up

Each of the scenes that follow consists of the modern text with commentary, as well as select speeches from the First Folio, which will include the background on the speech and other information including number of lines, approximate timing, and who is addressed.

PROBABLE TIMING: Shown on the page before the speech begins. 0.45 = a forty-five-second speech

Symbols & Abbreviations in the Commentary and Text

F: the First Folio

mt.: modern texts

F # followed by a number: the number of the sentence under discussion in the First Folio version of the speech; thus F #7 would refer to the seventh sentence

mt. # followed by a number: the number of the sentence under discussion in the modern text version of the speech, thus mt. #5 would refer to the fifth sentence

 # /# (e.g., 3/7): the first number refers to the number of capital letters in the passage under discussion; the second refers to the number of long spellings therein

/ within a quotation from the speech, the "/" symbol indicates where one verse line ends and a fresh one starts

[ ] : set around words in both texts when F1 sets one word, mt another

{ } : some minor alteration has been made, in a speech built up, where a word or phrase will be changed, added, or removed

{†} : this symbol shows where a sizable part of the text is omitted

Terms Found in the Commentary

OVERALL

1. **orthography:** the capitalization, spellings, punctuation of the First Folio

SIGNS OF IMPORTANT DISCOVERIES/ARGUMENTS WITHIN A FIRST FOLIO SPEECH

2. **major punctuation**: colons and semicolons: since the Shakespeare texts are based so much on the art of debate and argument, the importance of F1's major punctuation must not be underestimated, for both the semicolon (;) and colon (:) mark a moment of importance for the character, either for itself, as a moment of discovery or revelation, or as a key point in a discussion, argument, or debate that it wishes to impress upon other characters onstage.

As a rule of thumb:

a. the more frequent colon (:) suggests that whatever the power of the point discovered or argued, the character is not sidetracked and can continue with the argument—as such, the colon can be regarded as a **logical** connection

b. the far less frequent semicolon (;) suggests that because of the power inherent in the point discovered or argued, the character is sidetracked and momentarily loses the argument and falls back into itself or can only continue the argument with great difficulty—as such, the semicolon should be regarded as an **emotional** connection

3. **surround phrases**: phrase(s) surrounded by major punctuation, or a combination of major punctuation and the end or beginning of a sentence: thus these phrases seem to be of special importance for both character and speech, well worth exploring as key to the argument made and/or emotions released

A LOOSE RULE OF THUMB TO THE THINKING PROCESS OF A FIRST FOLIO CHARACTER

1. mental discipline/**intellect**: a section where capitals dominate suggests that the intellectual reasoning behind what is being spoken or discovered is of more concern than the personal response beneath it

2. feelings/**emotions**: a section where long spellings dominate suggests that the personal response to what is being spoken or discovered is of more concern than the intellectual reasoning behind it

3. **passion**: a section where both long spellings and capitals are present in almost equal proportions suggests that mind and emotion/feelings are inseparable, and thus the character is speaking passionately

SIGNS OF LESS THAN GRAMMATICAL THINKING WITHIN A FIRST FOLIO SPEECH

1. **onrush**: sometimes thoughts are coming so fast that several topics are joined together as one long sentence, suggesting that the F character's mind is working very quickly, or that his/her emotional state is causing some concern. Most modern texts split such a sentence into several grammatically correct parts (the opening speech of *As You Like It* is a fine example, where F's long eighteen-line opening sentence is split into six), while the modern texts' resetting may be syntactically correct, the F moment is nowhere near as calm as the revisions suggest.

2. **fastlink**: sometimes F shows thoughts moving so quickly for a character that the connecting punctuation between disparate topics is merely a comma, suggesting that there is virtually no pause in springing from one idea to the next. Unfortunately, most modern texts rarely allow this to stand, instead replacing the obviously disturbed comma with a grammatical period, once more creating calm that it seems the original texts never intended to show.

FIRST FOLIO SIGNS OF WHEN VERBAL GAME PLAYING HAS TO STOP

1. **nonembellished**: a section with neither capitals nor long spellings suggests that what is being discovered or spoken is so important to the character that there is no time to guss it up with vocal or mental excesses: an unusual moment of self-control.

2. **short sentence**: coming out of a society where debate was second nature, many of Shakespeare's characters speak in long sentences in which ideas are stated, explored, redefined, and summarized, all before moving on to the next idea in the argument, discovery, or debate. The longer sentence is the sign of a rhetorically trained mind used to public speaking (oratory), but at times an idea or discovery is so startling or inevitable that length is either unnecessary or impossible to maintain: hence the occasional very important short sentence suggests that there is no time for the niceties of oratorical adornment with which to sugar the pill—verbal games are at an end, and now the basic core of the issue must be faced.

3. **monosyllabic**: with English being composed of two strands, the polysyllabic (stemming from French, Italian, Latin, and Greek), and

the monosyllabic (from the Anglo-Saxon), each strand has two distinct functions: the polysyllabic words are often used when there is time for fanciful elaboration and rich description (which could be described as "excessive rhetoric") while the monosyllabic occur when, literally, there is no other way of putting a basic question or comment: Juliet's "Do you love me? I know thou wilt say aye" is a classic example of both monosyllables and non-embellishment. With monosyllables, only the naked truth is being spoken; nothing is hidden.

A Note on Magic, Ritual, & Incantation

In *The Tempest* magic is used in speeches of Prospero, Ariel, and Caliban.

The Patterns of "Normal" Conversation

The normal pattern of a regular Shakespearean verse line is akin to five pairs of human heartbeats, with ten syllables being arranged in five pairs of beats, each pair alternating a pattern of a weak stress followed by a strong stress. Thus, a normal ten-syllable heartbeat line (with the emphasis on the capitalized words) would read as

> weak - STRONG, weak - STRONG, weak - STRONG, weak - STRONG, weak - STRONG
> (shall I com- PARE thee TO a SUMM- ers DAY)

Breaks would either be in length (under or over ten syllables) or in rhythm (any combinations of stresses other than the five pairs of weak-strong as shown above), or both together.

The Patterns of Magic, Ritual, and Incantation

Whenever magic is used in the Shakespeare plays, the form of the spoken verse changes markedly in two ways. The length is usually reduced from ten to just seven syllables, and the pattern of stresses is completely reversed, as if the heartbeat was being forced either by the circumstances of the scene or by the need of the speaker to completely change direction. Thus in comparison to the normal line shown above, or even the occasional minor break, the more tortured and even dangerous magic or ritual line would read as

> STRONG - weak, STRONG- weak, STRONG - weak, STRONG
> (WHEN shall WE three MEET a GAINE)

The strain would be even more severely felt in an extended passage, as when the three wayward Sisters begin the potion that will fetch Macbeth to them. Again, the spoken emphasis is on the capitalized words and the effort of, and/or fixed determination in, speaking can clearly be felt.

> THRICE the BRINDed CAT hath MEW'D
> THRICE and ONCE the HEDGE-Pigge WHIN'D
> HARPier CRIES, 'tis TIME, 'tis TIME.

Unusual Aspects of Magic

It's not always easy for the characters to maintain it. And the magic doesn't always come when the character expects it. What is even more interesting is that while the pattern is found a lot in the Comedies, it is usually in much gentler situations, often in songs *(Two Gentlemen of Verona, Merry Wives of Windsor, Much Ado About Nothing, Twelfth Night, The Winter's Tale)* and/or simplistic poetry *(Love's Labour's Lost* and *As You Like It)*, as well as the casket sequence in *The Merchant of Venice*.

It's easy to dismiss these settings as inferior poetry known as doggerel. But this may be doing the moment and the character a great disservice. The language may be simplistic, but the passion and the magical/ritual intent behind it is wonderfully sincere. It's not just a matter of magic for the sake of magic, as with Puck and Oberon enchanting mortals and Titania in *A Midsummer Night's Dream*. It's a matter of the human heart's desires, too. Orlando, in *As You Like It*, when writing paeans of praise to Rosalind, suggests that she is composed of the best parts of the mythical heroines:

> THEREfore HEAVen NATure CHARG'D
> THAT one BODie SHOULD be FILL'D
> WITH all GRACes WIDE enLARG'D

And what could be better than Autolycus *(The Winter's Tale)* using magic in his opening song as an extra enticement to trap the unwary into buying all his peddler's goods, ballads, and trinkets?

SCENE STUDY

Act II, Scene i

Sebastian and Antonio

☙❧

After attending the wedding of his daughter in Tunis, Alonso, King of Naples, has been shipwrecked together with his entire court. Only his son and heir, Ferdinand, is missing and the others, keeping together for safety's sake, have been searching for him. They have become increasingly aware that something very unusual is happening, for they are all entirely unscathed by their adventure and their clothes look, if anything, "fresher than before." Moreover they have felt, quite suddenly, very tired and all at the same time have fallen asleep on the ground—all except Sebastian and Antonio.

These two are both younger brothers. Antonio had usurped the power of his elder brother years ago, and had set him adrift at sea accompanied by his infant daughter; since then he has reigned as Duke of Milan. Sebastian's older brother is Alonso, who is the king sleeping at his feet.

For this scene, four or more sleeping bodies are required but these can be supplied by pillows, boxes, rolls of material, or whatever is conveniently at hand. One such "body" should be identified as the king's, and another as Gonzalo's—he is a very senior court politician.

Swords are needed for this scene, in scabbards.

SEBASTIAN
   What a strange drowsiness possesses them!

ANTONIO
   It is the quality o' th' climate.

SEBASTIAN   Why
   Doth it not then our eyelids sink? I find not
   Myself disposed to sleep.

ANTONIO   Nor I: my spirits are nimble.

>   They fell together all, as by consent; 5
>   They dropped as by a thunderstroke. What might
>   Worthy Sebastian? O what might!— No more!—
>   And yet methinks I see it in thy face,
>   What thou shouldst be. Th' occasion speaks thee and
>   My strong imagination sees a crown 10
>   Dropping upon thy head.

SEBASTIAN   What? Art thou waking?

ANTONIO
>   Do you not hear me speak?

SEBASTIAN   I do and surely
>   It is a sleepy language and thou speak'st
>   Out of thy sleep. What is it thou didst say?
>   This is a strange repose, to be asleep 15
>   With eyes wide open, standing, speaking, moving
>   And yet so fast asleep.

ANTONIO   Noble Sebastian,
>   Thou let'st thy fortune sleep-die rather-wink'st
>   While thou art waking.

SEBASTIAN   Thou dost snore distinctly;
>   There's meaning in thy snores. 20

ANTONIO
>   I am more serious than my custom. You
>   Must be so too, if heed me; which to do
>   Trebles thee o'er.

SEBASTIAN   Well I am standing water.

ANTONIO
>   I'll teach you how to flow.

---

5 **consent** agreement
9 **speaks** calls to action / testifies to
18 **wink'st** hast thine eyes closed
22 **if heed** if you heed
23 **Trebles thee o'er** increases your fortunes threefold

Act II, Scene i (Sebastian and Antonio)

SEBASTIAN   Do so. To ebb
Hereditary sloth instructs me.   25

ANTONIO   O
If you but knew how you the purpose cherish
Whiles thus you mock it, how, in stripping it,
You more invest it! Ebbing men indeed
Must often do so near the bottom run
By their own fear or sloth.   30

SEBASTIAN   Prithee say on.
The setting of thine eye and cheek proclaim
A matter from thee and a birth indeed
Which throes thee much to yield.

ANTONIO   Thus sir:
Although this lord of weak remembrance, this
Who shall be of as little memory   35
When he is earthed, hath here almost persuaded
(For he's a spirit of persuasion, only
Professes to persuade) the king his son's alive,
'Tis as impossible that he's undrowned
As he that sleeps here swims.   40

SEBASTIAN   I have no hope
That he's undrowned.

ANTONIO   O out of that "no hope"
What great hope have you! No hope that way is

---

25 **hereditary sloth** inherited laziness, being born a younger son
26 **purpose** proposal
28 **invest** (1) clothe (2) give (royal) power to
29 **so near…run** i.e., their fortunes touch rock bottom
30 **Prithee** pray, please
31 **setting** fixed expression
32 **matter** theme of importance
33 **throes** pains (pun on **matter** = pus)
34 **weak remembrance** failing memory
36 **earthed** buried
38 **Profess to persuade** (1) has the profession of councilor (2) argues to argue

Another way so high a hope that even
  Ambition cannot pierce a wink beyond
  But doubt discovery there. Will you grant with me 45
  That Ferdinand is drowned?

SEBASTIAN　　　　　　　　He's gone.

ANTONIO　　　　　　　　Then tell me
  Who's the next heir of Naples?

SEBASTIAN　　　　　　　　Claribel.

ANTONIO
  She that is Queen of Tunis, she that dwells
  Ten leagues beyond a man's life, she that from Naples
  Can have no note—unless the sun were post; 50
  The man i' th' moon's too slow—till newborn chins
  Be rough and razorable; she that from whom
  We all were sea-swallowed, though some cast again,
  And by that destiny to perform an act
  Whereof what's past is prologue, what to come 55
  In yours and my discharge.

SEBASTIAN　　　　　　　　What stuff is this? How say you?
  'Tis true my brother's daughter's Queen of Tunis,
  So is she heir of Naples; twixt which regions
  There is some space.

---

44 **wink** glimpse
45 **doubt discovery** distrust what it sees
49 **man's life** i.e., a lifetime's journey
50 **note** information; **post** messenger
53 **sea-swallowed** drowned; **cast** thrown on shore (pun on **cast** = throw of dice)
54 **perform** (pun on casting a play; see l. 53)
56 **discharge** (1) execution (2) performance
59 **cubit** (about twenty inches)

Act II, Scene i (Sebastian and Antonio)

ANTONIO   A space whose ev'ry cubit
　Seems to cry out, "How shall that Claribel   60
　Measure us back to Naples? Keep in Tunis
　And let Sebastian wake!" Say this were death
　That now hath seized them, why they were no worse
　Than now they are. There be that can rule Naples
　As well as he that sleeps, lords that can prate   65
　As amply and unecessarily
　As this Gonzalo—! myself could make
　A chough of as deep chat. O that you bore
　The mind that I do, what a sleep were this
　For your advancement! Do you understand me?   70

SEBASTIAN
　Methinks I do.

ANTONIO   And how does your content
　Tender your own good fortune?

SEBASTIAN   I remember
　You did supplant your brother Prospero.

ANTONIO   True.
　And look how well my garments sit upon me
　Much feater than before. My brother's servants   75
　Were then my fellows, now they are my men.

SEBASTIAN
　But for your conscience—

ANTONIO
　Ay sir, where lies that? If 'twere a kibe,

61　**Measure us** travel to us
68　**chough ... chat** jackdaw to chatter as gravely as he
71　**content** understanding
72　**Tender** regard, take care of
75　**feater** more trimly
78　**kibe** blister on the heel

        'Twould put me to my slipper, but I feel not
        This deity in my bosom. Twenty consciences   80
        That stand 'twixt me and Milan, candied be they
        And melt, ere they molest! Here lies your brother,
        No better than the earth he lies upon—
        If he were that which now he's like, that's dead—
        Whom I with this obedient steel (three inches of it)   85
        Can lay to bed forever; whiles you, doing thus,
        To the perpetual wink for aye might put
        This ancient morsel, this Sir Prudence, who
        Should not upbraid our course. For all the rest,
        They'll take suggestion as a cat laps milk;   90
        They'll tell the clock to any business that
        We say befits the hour.

SEBASTIAN   Thy case, dear friend,
        Shall be my precedent. As thou got'st Milan,
        I'll come by Naples. Draw thy sword. One stroke
        Shall free thee from the tribute which thou payest   95
        And I the king shall love thee.

ANTONIO   Draw together
        And when I rear my hand, do you the like
        To fall it on Gonzalo.

SEBASTIAN   O but one word!

---

81 **candied** sugared, flattered
82 **molest** cause trouble
87 **wink** closed eye (i.e., sleep)
90 **suggestion** temptation
91 **tell the clock** (1) count the strokes of the clock (2) agree
98 **one word** i.e., one thing more

Rehearsing the Scene

Although Antonio takes the initiative, it would be a mistake to assume that he alone drives the scene forward. Sebastian is a practiced politician and knows how to play the waiting game to his own advantage; he is also the first one to look carefully at the sleeping bodies.

Antonio is very careful in raising the subject of assassination: see, for example, the complicated syntax and active wit of his speech, once Sebastian has indicated he is ready to listen (ll. 33–40). It is quite possible for Sebastian to be the one in control, his reference to his own "sloth" (l. 25) being only a pretense at aristocratic laziness and self-deprecation, designed to ensure that Antonio commits himself first.

Antonio speaks of his own "strong imagination" (l. 10) and this can be a useful clue for the actor. However concerned Antonio may be not to wake the sleepers and not to speak before time, Sebastian can see by the "setting" of his eye that he is in the grip of some idea that matters a great deal to him (ll. 31–33). When Antonio alludes for the first time to what must be done, his theatrical and godlike summons (ll. 54–56), springing out of a sharper, more everyday wit, can resound with imaginative power. Sebastian remains cool, and perhaps critical of this excess, but Antonio's mind is now racing ahead. The actor should resist making the proposal of murder too simple and enthusiastic: Antonio is able at this crisis to manage neat mimicry as a preface for his first use of the word "death," which is slipped in and then followed by a judicious touch of flattery (ll. 62–65). In contrast, Sebastian answers the summons carefully and briefly, "Methinks I do" (l. 71); and, when pressed to be more specific, challenges Antonio to commit himself. Probably this is the point where Antonio knows he has won, for he answers briskly and confidently (ll. 73–77).

But here is a critical juncture for both actors and an indication of how much can be presented subtextually in this scene. Having both played a very clever game of probing and concealment, searching behind words and appearances, now they may confront a major issue with the minimum of fuss, perhaps in a silence. As at lines 54–56, Antonio's reassuring words (ll. 74–76) echo now some words from *Macbeth* (I.iii and V.ii) concerned with the murder of Duncan: are these men, like Macbeth, responding to fear as well as to ambition? "But for your conscience" (l. 77) is an incomplete verse line and in the silence which follows the two may face the full consequences of murder. Antonio continues in a lighter vein, perhaps a sign that he fights to put fear behind him.

At this time the bodies should be very real to both characters. And a strange delay occurs, for although Sebastian says "Draw thy sword" (l. 94), Antonio's "Draw together" two lines later shows that neither acts at once. The scene will be very, very quiet; perhaps the breathing of the sleepers becomes audible. They have indeed been "snoring," according to Ariel, who will enter later to waken them (see II.i.304). Perhaps neither of them has drawn before Sebastian's "O but one word!"

Sebastian's last words seem to come from nowhere, and that might be intentional: perhaps they should be a response to strange and harsh sounds accompanying the arrival of the spirit Ariel, who has been sent by Prospero, the lord of the island, a magician and the former Duke of Milan, and who will wake the sleepers immediately after Sebastian has spoken. But Sebastian may well have questions to raise: Why does Antonio leave to him the secondary job of killing Gonzalo? How can Sebastian be sure he will not be blackmailed? Why not at least try to kill all the courtiers? If a strong subtextual energy has been created earlier, the actor should be able to find plenty of motive for a lastminute stall.

On a verbal level this scene is straightforward and intermittently witty, but to play the reality of two men preparing to murder—and, perhaps more difficult, to trust each other—is not at all easy.

First Folio Speech

For another perspective, following is a speech from this scene from the First Folio with commentary by Neil Freeman drawn from the *Once More Unto the Speech* series.

ANTHONIO {I} DID SUPPLANT {MY} BROTHER PROSPERO,

Background: Whatever his own agenda (probably to stop paying tribute to Alonso for his help in supplanting Prospero), Anthonio seems hell-bent on persuading Sebastian, Alonso's younger brother, to oust Alonso as King of Naples, just as he, Anthonio, usurped Prospero's throne. One note: line 17's "Sir Prudence" is a belittling term for Gonzalo. The use of curly brackets {} and {ψ} indicates where lines are cut or consolidated to make the speech work as a monologue.

Act II, Scene i (Sebastian and Antonio) 51

Style: as part of a two-handed scene in front of a larger sleeping group

Where: unspecified, somewhere on the island

To Whom: Sebastian, in front of the sleeping Alonso, Gonzalo, Adrian, Francisco, and unspecified "others"

# of Lines: 22 **Probable Timing:** 1.10 minutes

Anthonio

1   {ψ}   {I} did supplant {my} Brother Prospero {,}
           And looke how well my Garments sit upon me,
           Much feater [then] before : My Brothers servants
           Were then my fellowes, now they are my men .

2   {ψ}   {As for my} conscience {,}
    {ψ}   I Sir : where lies that ?

3   If 'twere a kybe
           'Twould put me to my slipper : But I feele not
           This Deity in my bosome : 'Twentie consciences
           That stand 'twixt me, and Millaine, candied be they,
           And melt ere they mollest :   Heere lies your Brother,
           No better [then] the earth he lies upon,
           If he were that which now hee's like (that's dead)
           Whom I with this obedient steele (three inches of it)
           Can lay to bed for ever : whiles you doing thus,
           To the perpetuall winke for aye might put
           This ancient morsell : this Sir Prudence, who
           Should not upbraid our course : for all the rest
           They'l take suggestion, as a Cat laps milke,
           They'l tell the clocke, to any businesse that
           We say befits the houre .

---

4   Draw together :
    And when I reare my hand, do you the like
    To fall it on Gonzalo .

Here Anthonio presents a very interesting method of persuasive attack to get what he needs: a sudden flurry of surround phrases to introduce or fortify the point he wants accepted, and then he relaxes somewhat so the other person can seemingly make their own decision.

- Thus, at the end of F #1 through to the third line of F #3, five successive surround phrases/lines convey the idea that conscience need not get in the way of absolute power:

> " : My Brothers servants / Were then my fellowes, now they are my men . As for my conscience, / I Sir : where lies that ? If 'twere a kybe / 'Twould put me to my slipper : But I feele not / This Deity in my bosome : "

- And in F #3, two more phrases speak to his need to get rid of Gonzalo:

> " : whiles you doing thus, / To the perpetuall winke for aye might put / This ancient morsell : this Sir Prudence, who / Should not upbraid our course : "

- In his attempt to seduce Sebastian, Anthonio gets straight to the point with a highly intellectual description of seizing and enjoying power (5/2, F #1).

- F #2's dismissal of "conscience" starts a little more carefully, via a careful short sentence (1/0) composed of surround phrases; but having begun to put aside Sebastian's possible objection and potential fear, Anthonio swiftly moves into overwhelm mode as he disavows any possibility of such an abstract notion standing "'twixt me, and Millaine." Passionate intellect and emotion are hard at work for F #3's first four and half lines (6/4).

- Introducing the idea of killing both King Alonso (Sebastian's brother) and his advisor Gonzalo ("This ancient morsell"), Anthonio becomes totally emotional (0/5 the next five and half lines), though his further scornful description of Gonzalo as "Sir Prudence" becomes momentarily intellectual (2/0) . . .

- . . . while his dismissal of the remainder as taking "suggestion, as a Cat laps milke" turns emotional once more (1/4, the last three lines of F #3).

- And, apparently having succeeded in moving Sebastian to action, the last sentence becomes careful (1/1, F #4), the first phrase containing a moment of emotional encouragement to strike (via the word "reare"), the second one of specific fact (directing Sebastian's murderous act towards "Gonzalo").

WORKING ON MODERN AND FIRST FOLIO TEXTS

Paul Sugarman

It is important when working on text that you gain information from modern edited texts, such as the Applause Shakespeare Library, which can provide much information on understanding what is happening in the scene, and then look at the original printed texts of the First Folio, such as the Applause First Folio Editions, which can give additional insights.

So on the pages that follow, we look at several of the key moments in the play, including Miranda's confrontation with Prospero following the tempest, Caliban's observation of Trinculo, and Ferdinand wooing Miranda as Prospero looks on. We first look at them as they appear in the Applause Shakespeare Library and then as rendered in *Once More Unto the Speech* by Neil Freeman.

Act I, Scene ii: Modern Text

Enter PROSPERO and MIRANDA.

MIRANDA If by your art,° my dearest father, you have
Put the wild waters in this roar, allay them.
The sky, it seems, would pour down stinking pitch,
But that the sea, mounting to th' welkin's cheek,°
Dashes the fire out. O, I have suffered 5
With those that I saw suffer: a brave° vessel,
Who had, no doubt, some noble creature in her,
Dashed all to pieces. O the cry did knock
Against my very heart. Poor souls, they perished.
Had I been any god of power, I would 10
Have sunk the sea within the earth or ere°
It should the good ship so have swallowed and
The fraughting° souls within her.

PROSPERO   I pray thee, mark me.—
I, thus neglecting worldly ends, all dedicated 90
To closeness° and the bettering of my mind
With that which, but by being so retired,
O'erprized all popular rate,° in my false brother
Awaked an evil nature; and my trust,
Like a good parent, did beget° of him 95
A falsehood in its contrary as great
As my trust was; which had indeed no limit,
A confidence sans° bound. He being thus lorded,°
Not only with what my revenue yielded,
But what my power might else exact, like one 100
Who having into truth, by telling of it,
Made such a sinner of his memory,
To credit his own lie,° he did believe
He was indeed the duke; out o' th' substitution°
And executing the outward face of royalty, 105
With all prerogative.°
Hence his ambition growing—Dost thou hear?

MIRANDA Your tale, sir, would cure deafness.

PROSPERO To have no screen° between this part he played
And him he played it for, he needs will be 110

Act I, Scene ii (Prospero, Miranda, Ariel)   55

| | **1–13** As noise of the storm continues offstage (at least until l. 5), Prospero is seen silent and probably quite still. (In Jacobean theaters he was probably "discovered" by drawing back a curtain from an inner or upper part of the stage.) The contrast with the frightened mariners and courtiers is extreme. He may hold his magic staff in outstretched hand, in charge of the tempest and then of the new silence. |

magical power

face of the sky

fine

before

conveyed as freight

seclusion

public, ordinary
   consideration
(proverbial saying "trust is
   the mother of deceit")

without   made a lord
who lies so constantly that he
   believes his own lie and so
   sins further against truth
(*into* = *unto*; *to* = as to)

in consequence of being
   my deputy
rights and privileges

division

The storm, however, is echoed in Miranda's words and her tears. Prospero does not reply to "my dearest father" and so she may turn away and the rest of her speech be a soliloquy. Certainly she is torn by contrary reactions, changing from trying to understand what she sees and what she imagines, to direct expression of her own suffering and her sympathy for others. Her thoughts settle (as more sustained rhythm and syntax indicate) only when she realizes what she would have done had she possessed the power of a "god." The audience, still knowing little of the situation, may sense that Prospero, clothed in his magic robe, is indeed a "god of power", and implacable.

90–109 Prospero goes back to the beginning of his tale, longer phrasing suggesting a slower pace. But complicated syntax and word order (the initial "I" governing the main verb, "Awaked", four lines later) with second thoughts and explanations all suggest care and deliberation: he is retelling the story so that all possible blame is placed on his own actions—it is his "trust" that awoke "evil."

As thoughts of Antonio's treachery possess his mind (l. 106) the incomplete verse-line suggests that he stops, his unspoken thoughts occupying his mind. Perhaps he thinks now of his own prerogative gained by a more than royal art—his power, already manifested in the tempest, by which he will exactly revenge and restitution. But starting once more, he breaks off to turn more gently to Miranda, as if to prove that he is in control of all elements of his tale. He pauses briefly again after his daughter's reply (note the incomplete line), but continues without break

Absolute Milan.° Me, poor man, my library
Was dukedom large enough: of temporal royalties°
He thinks me now incapable; confederates—
So dry he was for sway°—wi' th' King of Naples
To give him annual tribute, do him homage, 115
Subject his coronet to his crown and bend
The dukedom yet unbowed—alas, poor Milan!—
To most ignoble stooping.°

MIRANDA   O the heavens!

PROSPERO Mark his condition,° and th' event;° then tell me
If this might be a brother.

MIRANDA   I should sin 120
To think but° nobly of my grandmother:
Good wombs have borne bad sons.

PROSPERO   Now the condition:
The King of Naples, being an enemy
To me inveterate, hearkens my brother's suit,
Which was, that he, in lieu o' th' premises° 125
Of homage and I know not how much tribute,
Should presently° extirpate me and mine
Out of the dukedom and confer fair Milan
With all the honors, on my brother. Whereon,
A treacherous army levied, one midnight 130
Fated to th' purpose did Antonio open
The gates of Milan, and, i' th' dead of darkness,
The ministers° for the purpose hurried thence
Me and thy crying self.

MIRANDA   Alack, for pity!
I, not rememb'ring how I cried out then, 135
Will cry it o'er again: it is a hint°
That wrings° mine eyes to't.

PROSPERO   Hear a little further
And then I'll bring thee to the present business
Which now's upon's; without the which this story
Were most impertinent.°

MIRANDA   Wherefore did they not 140
That hour destroy us?

PROSPERO   Well demanded, wench:
My tale provokes that question. Dear, they durst not,

Act I, Scene ii (Prospero, Miranda, Ariel)

Duke of Milan in fact worldly royal duties	in his sense; he has almost bridged the gap that was between them.
he was so greedy for power	**110–140** Having named Antonio's ambition to be "Absolute Milan," Prospero once more becomes impassioned, expressing his thoughts with sarcastic irony and then a fourfold reiteration of the ignominious price Antonio paid for power. His rhetorical buildup is broken, however, by an instinctive "alas poor Milan," which is echoed by Miranda's less specific explanation (l. 118). He responds to her concern by asking her to judge rationally, insisting that she know the precise terms of his princedom's subjugation.
humiliation	
agreement, treaty consequence	
other than	
	Miranda, brought up on almost uninhabited island, is out of her depth: the nearest she can get to imagining the situation is to consider her grandmother and what she has been told about family histories. Prospero presses on without comment and starts to recall the coup d'etat more calmly.
in return for guarantees	
immediately	From political issues Prospero is drawn back into the actual drama of the particular night, investing it with hellish images as well as a sense of immediacy. With "Me and thy crying self," a new reality and feeling comes into a speech, a recollection of a young child's helplessness and of a tenderness that has outlasted the catastrophe. Miranda now weeps openly and can speak further only of her own inadequacy. This may well be the moment when Prospero sits down beside his daughter (he has taken this position by line 171); he continues more gently explaining that she must still be patient and attentive. He is also aware once more the time presses: he knows, throughout this difficult narration, that a crisis is upon him (see ll. 138–39). For this reason, perhaps, he had tried to tell her too much too soon, constantly asked her to pay strict attention, and here seems to cut her off with "Now the condition" (l. 122).
agents	
occasion forces	
pointless	
	140–45 Miranda's question shows that she is now more secure in her father's attention and presence. Prospero seems surprised momentarily by her grasp of

So dear the love my people bore me, nor set
A mark so bloody° on the business, but
With colors° fairer painted their foul ends. 145
In few,° they hurried us aboard a bark,
Bore us some leagues to sea, where they prepared
A rotten carcass of a butt,° not rigg'd,
Nor tackle, sail, nor mast; the very rats
Instinctively had quit it: there they hoist° us, 150
To cry to th' sea that roared to us, to sigh
To th' winds whose pity, sighing back again,
Did us but loving wrong.°

PROSPERO   Hast thou, spirit, 195
Performed to point° the tempest that I bade thee?

ARIEL To every article.
I boarded the king's ship; now on the beak,°
Now in the waist, the deck,° in every cabin,
I flamed amazement.° Sometime I'd divide, 200
And burn in many places; on the topmast,
The yards and boresprit° would I flame distinctly,°
Then meet and join. Jove's lightnings, the precursors
O' th' dreadful thunderclaps, more momentary
And sight-outrunning were not. The fire and cracks 205
Of sulfurous roaring the most mighty Neptune
Seem to besiege and make his bold waves tremble,
Yea, his dread trident shake.

PROSPERO   My brave° spirit!
Who was so firm, so constant, that this coil°
Would not infect his reason?

ARIEL   Not a soul 210
But felt a fever of the mad° and played
Some tricks of desperation.° All but mariners
Plunged in the foaming brine and quit the vessel,
Then all afire with me: the king's son, Ferdinand,
With hair up-staring,°—then like reeds, not hair,— 215
Was the first man that leap'd; cried, "Hell is empty,
And all the devils are here!"

Act I, Scene ii (Prospero, Miranda, Ariel)

(as hunters were *blooded* after killing a deer)
false appearances
briefly

tub

cast off

i.e., the winds blew only in sympathy with the fugitive's sighs

in every detail

pointed prow
poop
awoke terror by appearing as fire
bowsprit   separately

fine
turmoil

like madmen feel
strange reckless actions

standing on end

the situation, but he is more affectionate (see "wench" and "Dear" ll.141, 142); he proceeds more calmly with his tale and remembers "the love my people bore me."

(Antonio's decision to cast Prospero and Miranda adrift in a boat is the stuff of romantic fiction rather than political reality. By arranging the exposition so that Miranda's puzzlement is answered in a moment of mutual confidence and growing signs of affection, Shakespeare encourages a more ready acceptance of this circumstance by the theatre audience; it is pleased to follow where Miranda leads.)

195–197 Prospero's question about the "tempest" provides helpful exposition for the audience. Ariel's first short answer (l. 197) accentuates his quick, complete obedience and Prospero's power as "master." In a following pause, Prospero will seem to wait for, and so command, further information.

198–208 The rhythms of Ariel's narrative are alert and quick at first, but lengthen, probably in pleasure, as he describes the horror he has caused. He ends in the present tense, with a sense of immediacy; there is pride and amusement, or laughter, here.

Most Ariels mime or illustrate the event they describe: this gives an arresting impression to the spirit's first appearance; it also varies and enlivens the long exposition that Shakespeare's choice of a short time-span for the play's action has necessitated.

208–217 Although quick to show his pleasure to Ariel, Prospero reflects on the awful effects of the tempest he has raised, either delighting in the torture he inflicts or remembering his own suffering. It is probably the former, because Ariel continues brightly: he is not "human" and so does not sympathize with "tricks of desperation" in men; he may laugh or speak with mock sadness. Ferdinand's cry is, for Ariel, proof of his own adroitness; it is spoken in pride or with laughter, or with a consummate impression of high drama and seriousness undercut by exaggeration.

Act I, Scene ii: First Folio Speeches

MIRANDA   IF BY YOUR ART (MY DEEREST FATHER) YOU HAVE

Background: As her first speech in the play, chiding her father for creating such a dreadful tempest (see Ariel's speech further on below), it is self-explanatory.

Style: As the opening speech of a two-handed scene

Where: Unspecified, but somewhere close to her father's cell and close to Caliban's cave

To Whom: Her father Prospero

# of Lines: 13   **Probable Timing:** 0.45 minutes

Miranda

1   If by your Art (my deerest father) you have
     Put the wild waters in this Rore ; alay them :
     The skye it seemes would powre down stinking pitch,
     But that the Sea, mounting to th' welkins cheeke,
     Dashes the fire out .

2   Oh !

3   I have suffered
     With those that I saw suffer : A brave vessell
     (Who had   no doubt   some noble creature in her)
     Dash'd all to peeces :   O the cry did knocke
     Against my very heart : poore soules, they perish'd .

4   Had I byn any God of power, I would
     Have suncke the Sea within the Earth, or ere
     It should the good Ship so have swallow'd, and
     The fraughting Soules within her .

Initially, F's onrushed #1 and especially #3 would suggest a much less rational character than that which most modern texts present (all in all eight sentences to F's four). However, F's orthography shows Miranda growing before our eyes, moving through emotional concerns to a fine intellectual moral judgment—an essential and necessary step before

Act I, Scene ii (Prospero, Miranda, Ariel) 61

her father will expose her to the good of life (Ferdinand) after the bad (Caliban).

- It seems throughout the play that Miranda never masks her feelings, thus the opening two lines' surround phrases show her ability to stand up to her father for what she believes is right, and though the first line is passionate (1/1), she has sufficient self-control to not cloud the key second descriptive line and command (although the semicolon in " ; alay them : " suggests that emotions are not too far from the surface).

- However, after the command, she becomes highly emotional (1/4, the next two and a half lines of F #1–2) ending with a rare (for F) exclamation mark.

- That the opening of F #3 may not be just teenage hyperbole can be seen in the fact that her suffering is expressed as an unembellished surround phrase, and that the remaining three surround phrases which complete the sentence are filled with emotion (2/5, F #3's remaining three and a half lines).

- And then, through the pain, her intellect finally takes over as she takes a firm moral stand, preferring to destroy nature rather than sacrifice human life (5/3, F #4).

Prospero   I pray thee marke me :

Background: Faced with the prospect of dealing face to face with antagonists both past and present, Prospero begins to acquaint his daughter Miranda with the full details of how they have come to spend their last twelve years alone on the island they call home. In many ways she has demanded this, for the storm that Prospero has created to achieve his aims has disturbed her greatly (see the prior speech).

Style: Part of a two-handed scene.

Where: Unspecified, but somewhere close to their cell and close to Caliban's cave.

To Whom: His daughter Miranda

# of Lines: 42   **Probable Timing:** 2.00 minutes

Prospero

1 I pray thee marke me :
   I thus neglecting worldly ends, all dedicated
   To closenes, and the bettering of my mind
   with that, which but by being so retir'd
   Ore-priz'd all popular rate : in my false brother
   Awak'd an evill nature, and my trust
   Like a good parent, did beget of him
   A falsehood in it's contrarie, as great
   As my trust was, which had indeede no limit,
   A confidence sans bound .

2   He being thus Lorded,
   Not onely with what my revenew yeelded,
   But what my power might els exact .

3   Like one
   Who having into truth, by telling of it,
   Made such a synner of his memorie
   To credite his owne lie, he did beleeve
   He was indeed the Duke, out o'th' Substitution
   And executing th'outward face of Roialtie
   With all prerogative : hence his Ambition growing :
   Do'st thou heare ?

   _____

4 To have no Schreene between this part he plaid,
   And him he plaid it for, he needes will be
   Absolute Millaine, Me (poore man) my Librarie
   Was Dukedome large enough : of temporall royalties
   He thinks me now incapable .

Act I, Scene ii (Prospero, Miranda, Ariel) 63

5   Confederates
    (so drie he was for Sway) [with] King of Naples
    To give him Annuall tribute, doe him homage
    Subject his Coronet, to his Crowne and bend
    The Dukedom yet unbow'd (alas poore Millaine)
    To most ignoble stooping .

---

6   Marke his condition, and th'event, then tell me
     If this might be a brother .

---

7   This King of Naples being an Enemy
     To me inveterate, hearkens my Brothers suit :

Whereon
A treacherous Armie levied, one mid-night
Fated to th'purpose, did Anthonio open
The gates of Millaine, and ith' dead of darkenesse
The ministers for th'purpose hurried thence
Me, and thy crying selfe .

---

8   In few, they hurried us a-boord a Barke,
     Bore us some Leagues to Sea, where they prepared
     A rotten carkasse of a Butt, not rigg'd,
     Nor tackle, sayle, nor mast, the very rats
     Instinctively have quit it .

    That Prospero cannot deal with events objectively can be seen in the two ungrammatical periods (ending F #2 and #4); the way several sentences start out reported either calmly or intellectually and then move into emotion or passion; and the surround phrases urging Miranda to "marke" and "heare" him.

- It seems that the opening monosyllabic surround phrase " . I pray thee marke me : " has a great impact on Miranda (or perhaps himself, in confessing his negligence to his daughter), for the remainder of F #1's nine lines, dealing with how an "evill nature" awoke in his brother, are almost totally unembellished, establishing one of the longest calm passages in the later Shakespeare plays (0/2).

- However, as F #2's expansion of his brother "being thus Lorded" is touched upon, so his control begins to slip, both emotionally (1/3), and in the thinking process, for F adds a very strange ungrammatical period to end the thought, even though F #3 continues on with a much greater elaboration of Anthonio's growing beliefs and "Ambition"—a period never set by modern texts.

- And though ungrammatical, the period seems to mark a change with enormous implications for Prospero, for the elaboration shifts from the emotion of F #2 to passion in F #3 (4/5), the ending turning towards surround phrases once more, enhancing both the notion of " : hence his Ambition growing : " and the monosyllabic reinforcement of the need for Miranda to understand everything, " : Do'st thou heare ? "

- The expansion of Anthonio's "Ambition" becomes even more passionate (5/6 in the four and half lines of F #4), and equally troublesome to his logical presentation, for F #4 ends with yet another period most modern texts regard as ungrammatical—yet F's setting provides Prospero with a second break before he manages to establish some form of mental discipline in describing how Anthonio became "Confederates" with the "King of Naples" (F #5, 9/5): the needed break between F #4 and #5 coming with the (upsetting?) surround phrase of how Anthonio " : of temporall royalties / He thinks me now incapable . "

- Once more an instruction to Miranda, this time to "Marke his condition" (i.e., his brother's), is handled quite quietly (0/1, F #6) and, as before, at first he seems to be able to establish intellectual control, for F #7's first four-line description of his brother opening "The gates of Millaine" to "The King of Naples" (an "Enemy / To me inveterate") is strongly intellectual (7/1).

- And then F #7's final two-line recollection of himself and Miranda being hurried away "ith'dead of darkenesse" becomes emotional (0/2).

- The final description of the "rotten carkasse of a Butt" on to which they were hurried becomes passionate again (4/3, F #8)—though the last horrific recollection that the ship's condition was so bad "the very rats /

Instinctively have quit it" is unembellished, perhaps suggesting that the memory is almost too painful to talk about.

Ariel   To every Article.

Background: Prospero created the opening tempest (see Miranda's speech above) in order to both frighten and separate the various parties on-board so as to deal with them more easily. Ariel, Prospero's main confidant and chief controller of all the other spirits at his command, had some very specific tasks to perform without which Prospero's plans cannot come to fruition. The following is a response to Prospero's direct question "Hast thou, Spirit, / Perform'd to point, the Tempest that I bad thee".

Style: As part of a two-handed scene, with a third person sleeping on-stage.

Where: Unspecified, but somewhere close to Prospero's cell and close to Caliban's cave.

To Whom: Prospero, in front of the sleeping Miranda.

# of Lines: 19   **Probable Timing:** 1.00 minutes

Ariel

1   To every Article.

2   I boorded the Kings ship : now on the Beake,
    Now in the [Waste], the Decke, in every Cabyn,
    I flam'd amazement, sometime I'ld divide
    And burne in many places ; on the Top-mast,
    The Yards and Bore-spritt, would I flame distinctly,
    Then meete, and joyne.

3   Joves Lightning, the precursers
    O'th dreadfull Thunder-claps more momentarie
    And sight out-running were not ; the fire, and cracks
    Of sulphurous roaring, the most mighty Neptune
    Seeme to besiege, and make his bold waves tremble,
    Yea, his dread Trident shake.

4   Not a soule
    But felt a Feaver of the madde, and plaid
    Some tricks of desperation ; all but Mariners
    Plung'd in the foaming bryne, and quit the vessell ;
    Then all a fire with me the Kings sonne Ferdinand
    With haire up-staring (then like reeds, not haire)
    Was the first man that leapt ; cride hell is empty,
    And all the Divels are heere .

That Ariel is more a spirit of instant response and emotion rather than considered intellectual logic can be seen not simply in the releases throughout the speech, but also that, within the major punctuation, there are five emotional semicolons to just one colon, and just three surround phrases.

- After the very careful short F #1 reassuring Prospero he has done exactly as commanded (1/0), Ariel's reporting of the overall details is very passionate (8/10 in F #2's five and half lines . . .
- . . . while the vainglorious comparison of his own appearances to that of "Jove's Lightning" is somewhat more restrained, and slightly more intellectual than emotional (4/2, five and half lines of F #3).
- The surround phrases seem those of a triumphant (child-like?) story-teller—the first of which opens F #2 (logical thanks to the colon), announcing success (" . I boorded the Kings ship : "); the second is emotional (thanks to the semicolon), explaining how he kept safe the minor characters with no part to play in the ensuing unfolding of events (" ; all but Mariners / Plung'd in the foaming bryne, and quit the vessell ; "); the last, that ends the speech, deals with the successful separation of Ferdinand, who " ; cride hell is empty, / And all the Divels are heere . ", from those who are to be punished.

- Thus it's not surprising that the F #4 build-up to all but "Mariners" quitting the vessel because they all "felt a Feaver of the madde" is emotional (2/5), enhanced by two closely set emotional semicolons, and the description of Ferdinand's separation, one of the prime objectives he had to perform, also remains emotional (3/5, the last three and a half lines of the speech).

Act II, Scene i: Modern Text

GONZALO Had I plantation° of this isle, my lord—

ANTONIO He'd sow't with nettle-seed.°

SEBASTIAN Or docks, or mallows.

GONZALO And were the king on't, what would I do? 140

SEBASTIAN 'Scape being drunk for want of wine.

GONZALO I' th' commonwealth I would by contraries°
Execute all things. For no kind of traffic°
Would I admit; no name° of magistrate;
Letters° should not be known; riches, poverty, 145
And use of service,° none; contract, succession,°
Bourn,° bound° of land, tilth,° vineyard, none;
No use of metal, corn, or wine, or oil;
No occupation; all men idle, all;
And women too, but innocent and pure; 150
No sovereignty—

SEBASTIAN Yet he would be king on't.

ANTONIO The latter end of his commonwealth forgets the beginning.

GONZALO All things in common nature should produce
Without sweat or endeavor. Treason, felony, 155
Sword, pike, knife, gun, or need of any engine°
Would I not have; but nature should bring forth,
Of its own kind,° all foison,° all abundance,
To feed my innocent people.

SEBASTIAN No marrying 'mong his subjects? 160

Act II, Scene i (Gonzalo, Sebastian, Antonio)

With some hesitation, Gonzalo starts a new topic for conversation to keep the peace and take the king's thoughts off his grief. The mocking commentary starts up again, but he ignores it.

colonization

(pun on *plantation* = planting, sowing)

142–63 This passage is based on John Florio's translation of Montaigne's essay "Of the Cannibals." The piled-up description and emphatic negatives suggest a thoughtful energy of mind or a very zealous recital of ready-made opinion.

contrary to usual practice / by prohibitions
business
title
learning
serving a master / inheritance
boundary / enclosure / agriculture

Sebastian cuts in (l. 151) to point out a contradiction, but neither this nor laughter can silence Gonzalo now, or moderate his enthusiasm. Rather, he rises to a more general evocation of a Golden Age of fruitfulness and moral purity, such as poets imagined to have existed in an innocent past. Poets contemporary with Shakespeare shared this vision and they also imagined that the New World across the Atlantic offered opportunity to rediscover such a paradise; so Michael Drayton (1563–1631) praised Virginia, "Earth's only Paradise":

weapon
according to its own nature / plenty

Where Nature hath in store
Foul, venison, and fish,
And the fruitful'st soil
Without you toil,
Three harvests more,
All greater than your wish . . .

To whom the Golden Age
Still Nature's laws doth give,
No other cares attend,
But them to defend
From winter's rage,
That long there doth not live.

By the close of his account of plantation, Gonzalo holds the stage, usurping attention from Alonso; he may have forgotten whom he is addressing and be lost in his own fantasy. He does not refer to the king after line 138 until he hears the two lords claim that he is recommending freedom for "whores and knaves" (ll. 160-161).

ANTONIO None, man, all idle—whores and knaves.

GONZALO I would with such perfection govern, sir,
T' excel the Golden Age.°

Act II, Scene i (Gonzalo, Sebastian, Antonio)

mythical time of primitive perfection

An actor can make Gonzalo an enthusiastic revolutionary (although this does not agree with his deference elsewhere to authority), an idle talker, or fervent sentimentalist who enjoys day-dreaming about peace. Such a "Golden Age" is neither jest, dream, nor consolation, for Alonso; and having seen Prospero's kingdom, with its subject daughter, spirit and bestial insurgent, an audience may make further critical comparisons.

Gonzalo's sustained speech also marks, by contrast, the dispersed and nervous quality of the rest of the dialogue, his own included. Then it yields to renewed exchange of cheap sarcasm and recrimination.

Act II, Scene i: First Folio Text Speech

GONZALO **HAD I PLANTATION OF THIS ISLE MY LORD ,**

Background: Described by Prospero both as a "Noble Neopolitan" and "Holy Gonzalo," Gonzalo is doing anything he can to bring Alonso, the King of Naples, distraught at the apparent drowning death of his son Ferdinand, back into a sense of current reality and responsibility so as to unite the increasingly bickering and fragmented group (the two factions being the darker forces of Anthonio and Sebastian on the one hand, and the leaderless remainder, including "good" Gonzalo, on the other).

Style: One-on-one address in front of a larger group.

Where: Unspecified, somewhere on the island.

To Whom: Alonso, in front of Sebastian, Anthonio, Adrian and Francisco, and an unspecified number of "others."

# of Lines: 19 **Probable Timing:** 1.00 minutes

Gonzalo

1 Had I plantation of this Isle my Lord {,}

_____

   And were the King on't, what would I do ?

_____

2 I'th'Commonwealth I would (by contraries)
   Execute all things : For no kinde of Trafficke
   Would I admit : No name of Magistrate :
   Letters should not be knowne : Riches, poverty,
   And use of service, none : Contract, Succession,
   [Borne], bound of Land, Tilth, Vineyard none :
   No use of Mettall, Corne, or Wine, or Oyle :
   No occupation, all men idle, all :
   And Women too, but innocent and pure :
   No Soveraignty .

_____

3 All things in common Nature should produce
   Without sweat or endevour : Treason, fellony,

Act II, Scene i (Gonzalo, Sebastian, Antonio)   73

> Sword, Pike, Knife, Gun, or neede of any Engine
> Would I not have : but Nature should bring forth
> Of it owne kinde, all foyzon, all abundance
> To feed my innocent people .

---

4   I would with such perfection governe Sir :
    T'Excell the Golden Age .

This sequence is often played as one long, boring blab, yet F's orthography clearly shows a key difference in conception and realization between (the discoveries of?) F #2 and (the resultant reverie of) F #3.

• It seems that the opening monosyllabic surround phrase " . I pray thee marke me : " has a great impact on Miranda (or perhaps himself, in confessing his negligence to his daughter), for the remainder of F #1's nine.

• In trying to get Alonso's attention, Gonzalo opens quite intellectually (4/0, F #1 and the first line and half of F #2), but once the idea of ruling by "contraries" is voiced, so his pattern completely changes.

• The lengthy F #2 itemizing how this would work is composed entirely of ten surround phrases, and whether this is an attempt to get through to the distracted Alonso, or is indicative of his own mind running rampant with the somewhat revolutionary ideas (though modern editors suggest that this passage is meant as a criticism of the rather startling propositions of the French philosopher Montaigne) is up to each actor to decide.

• The first explorations in the denial-of-status-distinction ideas from "For no kinde of Trafficke / Would I admit" through to "And use of service, none" are passionate (4/3 in just three lines). Then, moving into concerns of business and the impact of the new order on human beings, Gonzalo becomes intellectual (11/3, the last five lines of F #2).

• And with F #3's utopian overview, the surround phrases, if such still can be said to exist, become much longer, and though the suggestion that "Nature" should be allowed to develop without "sweat or endevour" still remains intellectual (6/3, the first three and half lines of F #3), the shift into the idealistic hope that "Nature should bring forth / Of it owne kinde" becomes (delightedly?) emotional (1/3).

• F #4's intellectual character, surpassing the "Golden Age" finale (4/2), is heightened by being expressed once again via two surround phrases.

Act II, Scene ii: Modern Text

Enter CALIBAN with a burden of wood. A noise of thunder heard.

CALIBAN All the infections that the sun sucks up
From bogs, fens, flats,° on Prosper fall, and make him
By inchmeal° a disease! His spirits hear me
And yet I needs must curse. But they'll nor pinch,
Fright me with urchin shows,° pitch me i' the mire, 5
Nor lead me, like a firebrand, in the dark
Out of my way, unless he bid 'em. But
For every trifle are they set upon me;
Sometime like apes that mow° and chatter at me,
And after bite me; then like hedgehogs which 10
Lie tumbling in my barefoot way and mount
Their pricks at my footfall; sometime am I
All wound° with adders who with cloven tongues
Do hiss me into madness.

Enter Trinculo.

                    Lo, now, lo!
Here comes a spirit of his, and to torment me 15
For bringing wood in slowly. I'll fall flat;
Perchance he will not mind° me. *[Falls on the ground.]*

TRINCULO Here's neither bush nor shrub, to bear° off any weather
at all, and another storm brewing; I hear it sing i' the wind.
Yond same black cloud, yond huge one, looks like a foul bom- 20
bard° that would shed his liquor. If it should thunder as it did
before, I know not where to hide my head. Yond same cloud
cannot choose but fall by pailfuls. What have we here? a man or
a fish? Dead or alive? A fish. He smells like a fish; a very
ancient and fishlike smell; a kind of not of the newest Poor- 25
John.° A strange fish. Were I in England now, as once I was,
and had but this fish painted,° not a holiday fool there but

Act II, Scene ii (Caliban, Trinculo)   75

swamps little by little goblin sights pull faces coiled around	**1-17** In Jacobean public theaters thunder was an impressive sound effect that literally shook the wooden structure of the building. Here it follows immediately on the exits from the previous scene, shattering the silence; it is accompanied with lightning. Caliban's curse is heard after the thunder, as an answer or complement; usually he heaves the great log he bears in the air threateningly. After this only the wind is heard offstage (see l. 19), but it is enough for Caliban to cower in expectation of more punishment. He tells himself that he is overheard and that the slightest thing he does wrong will be punished, so after the rebellious curse he starts recalling nightmarish horrors, hoping they will not be inflected. Perhaps he tries to forestall punishment or talks only to keep up his courage. But the thought of Prospero's bidding stops any hope of escape and he starts enumerating tortures that are increasingly taunting and enveloping. A soliloquy which had started as defiance, angry, cruel, and resolved, concludes with imaginative suffering, crazed impotence, close to "madness" (l. 14).
notice ward	At the peak of Caliban's expectation of torture, a silent fool enters the back of the stage: the dispirited, fearful Trinculo. At once, perhaps comically, Caliban falls flat on the ground, all remnants of courage gone. He pulls "gaberdine" (l.35) over his shoulders so that it covers all but his extremities; he trembles and then manages to lie dead-still.

leather jug
 	
salted hake
(as a sign to attract
   customers to a booth at
   a fair)
	18-37 Trinculo wanders wearily around, looking for shelter, complaining and cowering as he observes a huge black cloud above his head. He seems to take some comfort in knowing that the is about to be drenched: the "cloud cannot choose" but afflict him (ll. 22-23). But as he believes he knows what will happen next, he trips over the prostrate Caliban, who shrinks and trembles at his touch and then lies absolutely still as if hoping to escape notice.
	
	Trinculo stands back in amazement and then fear. Gingerly, he questions, peers, smells, prods and,

would give a piece of silver.° There would this monster make
a man;° any strange beast there makes a man. When they will
not give a doit° to relieve a lame beggar, they will lazy out ten   30
to see a dead Indian. Legged like a man—and his fins like arms!
Warm,° o' my troth! I do now let loose my opinion; hold it no
longer: this is no fish, but an islander, that hath lately suffered
by a thunderbolt. *[Thunder]* Alas, the storm is come again! My
best way is to creep under his gaberdine°; there is no other   35
shelter hereabouts: misery acquaints a man with strange bedfel-
lows. I will here shroud till the dregs° of the storm be past.
[Creeps under Caliban's garment.]

Act II, Scene ii (Caliban, Trinculo)

(i.e., to see this fish)
Make a man's fortune /
  be taken for a man
  (wordplay on *monster*)
smallest coin
(a *fish* would be cold)

cloak

(wordplay on
  bombardment,
  lines 20–21)

finally, pronounces "A fish" (l. 24). If this does not raise a laugh, Caliban will by shrinking still further under his gaberdine.

Trinculo goes on sniffing and commenting, until he sees how this may turn to his own advantage; he soon warms to the idea of making his fortune. By "dead Indian" (l. 31), he has regained his courage and starts prodding his "strange beast" (l. 29) with more purpose. Comic business develops easily here as Trinculo slowly comes to recognize a fellow creature. He is about to investigate when another clap of thunder petrifies him (l. 34). He hurriedly takes shelter, pausing only to make his excuse and, usually, to hold his nose and shut his eyes. He attains a definitive shred of proverbial wisdom about "misery" (l. 36)—delivered with emphasis directly to the audience, it raises an inevitable laugh—and then plunges regardless of discomfort under the gaberdine: there is a commotion, and then all is dead-still.

As a traditional clown in a play, Trinculo talks directly to the audience in the theater, demonstrating to them and debating for them and with them. So, as Trinculo finds kinship with Caliban, the audience finds itself close to the fool, enjoying both his sad and his superior jokes and laughing at him, at Caliban and at the storm itself.

Act II, Scene ii: First Folio Speeches

CALIBAN   ALL THE INFECTIONS THAT THE SUNNE SUCKES UP

Background: Now gathering the wood as Prospero charged, and alone, Caliban gives vent to his feelings, presumably in part trying to win the audience to his side.

Style: Solo.

Where: Somewhere uninhabited on the island, possibly near the shore.

To Whom: Direct audience address.

# of Lines: 17   **Probable Timing:** 0.55 minutes

Caliban

1   All the infections that the Sunne suckes up
     From Bogs, Fens, Flats, on Prosper fall, and make him
     By ynch-meale a disease : his Spirits heare me,
     And yet I needes must curse .

2   But they'll nor pinch,
     Fright me with Urchyn-shewes, pitch me i'th mire,
     Nor lead me like a fire-brand, in the darke
     Out of my way, unlesse he bid'em; but
     For every trifle, are they set upon me,
     Sometime like Apes, that moe and chatter at me,
     And after bite me : then like Hedg-hogs, which
     Lye tumbling in my bare-foote way, and mount
     Their pricks at my foot-fall : sometime am I
     All wound with Adders, who with cloven tongues
     Doe hisse me into madnesse :

[Enter Trinculo]
                              Lo, now Lo,
     Here comes a Spirit of his, and to torment me
     For bringing wood in slowly : I'le fall flat,
     Perchance he will not minde me .

* Even though the first sentences match, thereafter F's single onrushed sentence shows a far more disturbed character than do the five sentences most

Act II, Scene ii (Caliban, Trinculo) 79

modern texts split it into, and F's orthography shows an interesting pattern in that after the opening passionate explosion (6/6), despite the onrushed F #2, Caliban begins to calm down and establish some form of self control.

- That Caliban can never be in full control is summed up in the surround phrase that ends F #1—": his Spirits heare me, / And yet I needes must curse . "—while the somewhat longer surround phrases that end the speech sum up both his fears and his response to danger: " : then like Hedg-hogs, which / Lye tumbling in my bare-foote way, and mount / Their pricks at my foot-fall : sometime am I / All wound with Adders, who with cloven tongues / Doe hisse me into madnesse : Lo, now Lo, / Here comes a Spirit of his, and to torment me /For bringing wood in slowly : I'le fall flat, / Perchance he will not minde me . "

- Caliban seems to want to present himself as a calm character, only to have this mask suddenly destroyed by bursts of release as with the emotional "Sunne suckes up" and the intellectual "Bogs, Fens, Flats, on Prosper fall" all in the first sentence, or the emotional "Doe hisse me into madnesse" and the intellectual " ; Lo, now Lo, / here comes a Spirit of his," in the second sentence.

- The explosion of the first sentence (6/6 in just three and a half lines) becomes more controlled, that is, with proportionately fewer releases (just 4/9 in F #2's first ten lines) but nevertheless emotional rather than intellectual in describing what Prospero's "Spirits" do to him—an attempt at gaining the audience's empathy / sympathy, perhaps?

- The (mistaken) realization that Prospero has sent another "Spirit" to torment him (in fact the character entering is the very human Trinculo, jester to Alonso) is intellectual (3/0), while the plan to avoid detection by falling "flat" is spoken very quietly (0/1), perhaps so as not to give himself away.

TRINCULO   HERE'S NEITHER BUSH, NOR SHRUB TO BEARE OFF ANY

Background: The first speech for one of the shipwrecked Neapolitans, Trinculo, jester to Alonso, who has just "swom ashore like a Ducke." Keeping in mind that the second sentence marks his discovery of the inadequately camouflaged Caliban, the speech is self-explanatory. Considering that F sets the speech as just two sentences, which most modern texts split into seventeen, it is suggested that the reader explore the stepping stones of the modern text first before trying to put F's onrush together, and even then, as an intermediary step, it might be worthwhile considering redividing F to match the modern text sentence structure as follows; mt. #1–5, the impending storm; #6–8, a man or a fish?; #9–11, how much money he could make in England; #12–14, the decision that this is "an Islander"; #15–16, what to do now that the storm's here; #17, the finale.

Style: Solo.

Where: On an open part of the island.

To Whom: Direct audience address.

# of Lines: 25   **Probable Timing:** 1.15 minutes

Trinculo

1   Here's neither bush, nor shrub to beare off any weather at all : and another Storme brewing, I heare it sing ith' winde : yond same blacke cloud, yond huge one, lookes like a foule bumbard that would shed his licquor : if it should thunder, as it did before, I know not where to hide my head : yond same cloud cannot choose but fall by paile-fuls .

2   What have we here, a man, or a fish ? dead or alive ? a fish, hee smels like a fish : a very ancient and fish-like smell : a kinde of, not of the newest poore-John : a strange fish : were I in England now (as once I was) and had but this fish painted ; not a holiday-foole there but would give a peece of silver : there, would this Monster, make a man : any strange beast there, makes a man : when they will not give a doit to relieve a lame Begger, they will lay out ten to see a dead Indian : Leg'd like a man ; and his Finnes like Armes : warme o'my troth : I doe now let loose my opinion ; hold it no longer ; this is no fish, but an Islander, that hath lately suffered by a Thunderbolt : Alas, the storme is come againe : my best way is to creepe under his Gaberdine : there is no other shelter hereabout : Misery acquaints a man with strange bedfellowes : I will here shrowd till the dregges of the storme be past .

Act II, Scene ii (Caliban, Trinculo) 81

That the onrushed speech is composed almost entirely of surround phrases (at least twenty-four) suggests a character who is working very hard to accommodate himself to the strangeness of his new surroundings, and it is not surprising that here Trinculo is more emotional than intellectual, having made his way from the shipwreck to the island, as he describes it later because he "swom ashore . . . like a Ducke".

- Accordingly, the fact of the storm coming (the modern texts' first three sentences) is emotional (1/8, the first four lines of the speech), especially marked by the two surround phrases that open the speech.

- And it may be that Trinculo is afraid of "thunder", for the remaining two and half lines of F #1 are completely unembellished save for the last word anticipating the awful amount of rain that is bounds to fall, "paile-fuls".

- He may also be frightened by the discovery of Caliban—"What have we here, a man or a fish ? dead or alive ? "—for not only is this opening of F #2 also unembellished and monosyllabic, as with F #1 it starts with two surround phrases.

- Caliban's smell (mt. #7) is responded to emotionally (1/3 in two lines), while the thought of having such a fish in England, leading to riches, becomes somewhat intellectual for the first time in the speech (4/2, the six lines equal to mt. 9–11).

- The final conjecture that Caliban might be "an Islander" felled by a "Thunderbolt", is passionate (5/4, the three line equivalent of mt. #12–14), though approaching Caliban to make this assessment may be somewhat disturbing for Trinculo, since there are three emotional semicolons set within the passage, affecting four of the six surround phrases the discovery / decision is couched in.

- Again, the approaching storm seems to disturb him, for the surround phrase—" : Alas, the storme is come againe : "—has three releases in six words (1/2).

- And while the initial decision, smell notwithstanding, to "creepe under his Gaberdine" for shelter / safety is passionate, the idea (and/or smell) may be repugnant to him, for the immediate follow-up is the unembellished surround phrase " : there is no other shelter hereabout : ", in turn succeeded by the somewhat heartfelt and released surround phrase maxim (1/1) " : Misery acquaints a man with strange bedfellowes : "

- The very last (surround) monosyllabic phrase becomes highly emotional—" : I will here shrowd till the dregges of the storme be past." (0/3)—though whether this signifies fear (of the storm), joy (at being partly sheltered), or disgust (at the smell) is up to each actor to decide.

Act III, Scene i: Modern Text

Enter FERDINAND, bearing a log.

FERDINAND There be some sports are painful, and their labour
Delight in them sets off.° Some kinds of baseness
Are nobly undergone, and most poor matters
Point to rich ends. This my mean° task
Would be as heavy to me as odious, but   5
The mistress which I serve quickens° what's dead
And makes my labors pleasures. O, she is
Ten times more gentle than her father's crabbed,
And he's composed of harshness. I must remove
Some thousands of these logs and pile them up,   10
Upon a sore injunction.° My sweet mistress
Weeps when she sees me work, and says, such baseness
Had never like executor. I forget;°
But these sweet thoughts do even refresh my labors,
Most busy least,° when I do it.

Enter MIRANDA; and PROSPERO at a distance, unseen.

MIRANDA Alas, now, pray you,   15
Work not so hard! I would the lightning had
Burnt up those logs that you are enjoined to pile!
Pray set it down, and rest you. When this burns,
'Twill weep for having wearied you. My father
Is hard at study; pray now, rest yourself.   20
He's safe for these three hours.

FERDINAND O most dear mistress,
The sun will set before I shall discharge
What I must strive to do.

MIRANDA   If you'll sit down,
I'll bear your logs the while. Pray, give me that;
I'll carry it to the pile.

FERDINAND   No, precious creature,   25
I had rather crack my sinews, break my back,
Than you should such dishonor undergo,
While I sit lazy by.

Act III, Scene i (Ferdinand, Miranda, Prospero) 83

1–15 Ferdinand's entry with a log echoes Caliban's in the previous scene and its manner contrasts with Caliban's exit immediately before. But there is no thunder and no curse.

Usually Ferdinand has stripped off his doublet and is disheveled and dirty; he may look more like Caliban in this servitude than had seemed conceivable.

> the trouble they cause makes the pleasure they give seem greater
> lowly

Setting down his log, Ferdinand tries to justify the "baseness" (l. 2) of his task, using short sentences suiting delivery between deeply drawn breaths as he recovers from his exertions. As soon as he remembers the "rich ends" for which he works, his vitality "quickens" (l. 6), and his rhythm and phrasing lengthen.

> gives life to

Even thoughts of Prospero's "harshness" reminds him of Miranda and he pictures her in his mind, remembering her loving words (ll. 11–13). He has to force himself to return to his "labors". At line 15, he again picks up the heavy log—and at this moment Miranda runs in. He turns to face her and stands holding the log, forgetting its weight completely.

> harsh directive
>
> i.e., my task

Both characters have awoken to a wholly unexpected experience. Surrounded with strange sounds on a mysterious island, made impotent by magic, encountering a seeming goddess and a harsh, unreasonable father, believing his own father drowned, Ferdinand nevertheless trusts his own feelings and sense of delight, beyond all ordinary discretion. Miranda, in a moment's recognition, has grown from girl to woman and has confronted her protective father to identify boldly with Ferdinand; she knows that she would use Prospero's control of the "lightning" (l. 16) very differently, and she has just escaped, as she thinks, from his surveillance for "three hours" (l. 21).

> busiest when most idle (because occupied with thoughts of love)

15–31 While Miranda goes to Ferdinand, Prospero stands at some distance behind her. He may be on an upper level of the stage, but if he is on the same level as the two lovers, the actor will be more able to show his reactions to them and his effort, perhaps to prevent himself interfering with what happens.

Ferdinand forgets his holding the log, and when Miranda tells him to "set it down" (l. 18) he does not do so, perhaps because he refuses to seem weak in her

MIRANDA   It would become me
As well as it does you; and I should do it
With much more ease, for my good will is to it,   30
And yours it is against.

PROSPERO   Poor worm, thou art infected!
This visitation° shows it.

MIRANDA   You look wearily.

FERDINAND No, noble mistress, 'tis fresh morning with me
When you are by at night. I do beseech you—
Chiefly that I might set it in my prayers—   35
What is your name?

MIRANDA   Miranda.—O my father,
I have broke your hest° to say so!

FERDINAND   Admired° Miranda!°
Indeed the top of admiration! worth
What's dearest to the world! Full many a lady
I have eyed with best regard,° and many a time   40
Th' harmony of their tongues hath into bondage
Brought my too diligent° ear. For several° virtues
Have I liked several women; never any
With so full soul but some defect in her
Did quarrel with the noblest grace she owed,°   45
And put it to the foil.° But you, O you,
So perfect and so peerless, are created
Of every creature's best.

MIRANDA   I do not know
One of my sex; no woman's face remember,
Save, from my glass, mine own. Nor have I seen   50
More that I may call men than you, good friend,
And my dear father. How features are abroad,
I am skilless° of; but by my modesty,
The jewel in my dower, I would not wish
Any companion in the world but you;   55
Nor can imagination form a shape,
Besides yourself, to like of. But I prattle
Something too wildly, and my father's precepts
I therein do forget.

FERDINAND   I am in my condition,°
A prince, Miranda; I do think, a king—   60

Act III, Scene i (Ferdinand, Miranda, Prospero)

eyes or unwilling to serve for her sake. After twice being asked to "rest," Ferdinand apologizes, with utmost reverence, and probably starts work once more.

Usually the log is so huge that Miranda's offer to "bear" it (l. 24) is absurd (her phrases are short, as if she is preparing to take the strain), and Ferdinand's refusal to say as much is ostentatiously gallant. He does, however, point out that he is under some strain himself. It is hard to know whether Miranda sees the joke in saying that the labor would "become" her (l. 28), but her point about good, or free "will" is shrewd, because he and not she has been ordered to do the work. By line 31, Ferdinand has put down the log.

visit (to Ferdinand) / attack of the plague / act of God

bidding
to be wondered at (Latin, *wonderful*)

attention, affection

heedful
different

possessed
overthrow it / offset it

ignorant

rank

When Prospero hears Miranda explain how she has made sure her father is "safe" for three hours (l. 21), he may step forward instinctively, or smile ironically; some Prosperos might turn away as if struggling to hold back from a confrontation.

31–32 Prospero's aside complicates the comedy. He may laugh in good humor, but he speaks of love as a sickness and so he could remain aloof from the feelings of the two young people, counting himself superior. At the other extreme, he could speak as if trying to devalue what he sees, being envious of it and knowing it to be beyond his own competence (see l. 92).

32–59 As Miranda sympathizes, Ferdinand, forgetting his weariness, asserts the ideal nature of his love. He begs to be told her name with an excuse to show that he is not being presumptuous. Miranda answers impulsively, but instantly remember her father's prohibition and probably draws back.

Ferdinan echoes her name, accepting it as a token both of trust and wonder. His whole "world" (l. 39) is revalued and, rather clumsily and at some length, he goes on to share his sense of the pettiness of all the women to whom he had previously paid attention. Perhaps he knows that he is saying too much and too little: he breaks off to exclaim on Miranda's perfection.

Miranda replies artlessly, speaking from her "imagination" (l. 56), with words tumbling out "something too wildly" (l. 58). She begins by admitting her

I would, not so!—and would no more endure
This wooden° slavery than to suffer
The flesh-fly blow° my mouth. Hear my soul speak:—
The very instant that I saw you, did
My heart fly to your service; there resides, 65
To make me slave to it; and for your sake
Am I this patient log-man.

MIRANDA   Do you love me?

FERDINAND O heaven, O earth, bear witness to this sound
And crown what I profess with kind event°
If I speak true! If hollowly,° invert 70
What best is boded me to mischief!° I,
Beyond all limit of what else i' th' world
Do love, prize, honor you.

MIRANDA   I am a fool
To weep at what I am glad of.

PROSPERO Fair encounter
Of two most rare affections! Heavens rain grace 75
On that which breeds between 'em!

FERDINAND   Wherefore weep you?

MIRANDA At mine unworthiness that dare not offer
What I desire to give, and much less take
What I shall die to want.° But this is trifling;
And all the more it seeks to hide itself, 80
The bigger bulk it shows. Hence, bashful cunning!
And prompt me, plain and holy innocence!
I am your wife, it you will marry me;
If not, I'll die your maid. To be your fellow°
You may deny me; but I'll be your servant, 85
Whether you will or no.

FERDINAND   My mistress, dearest,
And I thus humble ever.

MIRANDA   My husband, then?

FERDINAND Ay, with a heart as willing
As bondage e'er of freedom.° Here's my hand.°

MIRANDA And mine, with my heart in't; and now farewell, 90
Till half an hour hence.

FERDINAND A thousand thousand!°

Act III, Scene i (Ferdinand, Miranda, Prospero)

inferior / log-bearing
contaminate

contrasting inexperience, but so confidently that she links her new "good friend" with her "dear father", disregarding now the latter's opposition to Ferdinand and his denigration of her good opinion of him in I.ii. As she speaks of "modesty", her thoughts are also running to the "dower" to be given at her wedding. She tells Ferdinand that he is all she longs for, in mind and in body (see "shape", l. 56). By line 57 she has nothing left to say; she probably gazes as Ferdinand and then withdraws a little, aware once more of her father. Both lovers seem foolish at times in this encounter, but comedy need not confuse or mask the delicacy, strength, rapture and transforming nature of their feelings.

happy ending
falsely
turn to disaster the best
   that Fortune has in
   store for me

59–74 Ferdinand prepares to make a vow. He is thoughtful and sober, speaking of his inheritance without boasting and of his pride without implying that it is important. He calls her by her name (but does not use the word "love") and claims to serve her, without assuming acceptance. He hesitates only to speak of his father's death, and then to assure her that it is his soul that is engaged (l. 63).

lack

In reply, Miranda asks for love simply, without artifice or cautioning though (l. 67). With a still more solemn but more eager vow, Ferdinand pledges life. Before he has finished speaking, Miranda is weeping for joy: her feelings almost overwhelm her, so that in words she can only acknowledge that she is a "fool" (ll.73-74) unable to express herself.

equal

At line 68, Ferdinand probably kneels, and Miranda may too.

74–76 Prospero's second aside is wholly different from his first. He speaks in joy and admiration, and prays devoutly for the future. His nature, in any performance, will be clearly expressed at this point: does he move towards them, or turn away, or seem most concerned to pray for Heaven's help? How sure is he of their happiness; how much does he share in it? Almost certainly he does not spell-stop the lovers here.

as ever a slave is to be free
(as a bond of betrothal)

(farewells)

77–91 As Ferdinand show his sympathy and puzzlement, Miranda tries to speak of her love. In a

87

Exeunt FERDINAND and MIRANDA severally.

PROSPERO So glad of this as they I cannot be,
Who are surprised withal;° but my rejoicing
At nothing can be more. I'll to my book;°
For yet, ere suppertime, must I perform   95
Much business appertaining.   *[Exit.]*

at it
(of magic)

complicated way she tries to explain why she weeps, but very quickly she acknowledges this is "trifling" and "bashful cunning" (ll. 79-81). She decides to be more direct and offers herself as "wife" before he has asked (l. 83). Any alternative will leave her love unaltered; her fears of rejection tell her this—and she expresses these too. All these thoughts press hard, one after other.

Ferdinand answers simply, insisting still on his "humble" service. It is Miranda who uses the word "husband" first (l. 87), as she had introduced "wife." The incomplete verse-line (l. 88) indicates a pause—whether of wonder, pleasure, or disbelief—before Ferdinand's "Ay". He goes on to say that giving his hand in bond of marriage is release and freedom. They both pledge their faiths, probably kneeling together in a formal betrothal. It is a delicate and unruffled climax to the scene: inner content gives new strength and stability to words, and everything is still, including Prospero at some distance. Nothing so far in the play has established such a sense of peace and fulfillment.

But then, with no preparation or explanation, Miranda says "farewell" (l. 90); she probably runs off and Ferdinand calls after her. She may kiss him, and he may respond with many more; but the change of mood from the betrothal seems more sudden and sharp than this would imply. Both are radiant with happiness but break off their meeting rapidly, almost as if afraid to continue together, or as if summoned by another force. Possibly Prospero has exerted his power (as he did at the end of I.ii) and they have become, almost comically, something like robots doing his bidding. Ferdinand takes up his log without another word.

92–96 Prospero does not speak until the lovers have parted. He has been thinking of himself, as well as of them, and so there may be some irony in speaking of his "book" and "business", especially if Ferdinand can still be seen dragging his log offstage. It is a quiet, understated, and lonely end to the scene.

Prospero is not seen at this moment to be all-powerful, even though his plans are being successful; he must work to conform to a specific timetable, which he has not chosen (see l. 95).

Act III, Scene i: First Folio Speeches

FERDINAND THERE BE SOME SPORTS ARE PAINFULL ; & THEIR LABOR

Background: To test Ferdinand and Miranda's strength of affection for each other, Prospero has forced him, a prince unused to manual labor, to tidy up the wood that Caliban has brought. As such the speech is self-explanatory.

Style: Solo.

Where: Near to Prospero's cell.

To Whom: Direct audience address.

# of Lines: 16 **Probable Timing:** 0.50 minutes

Ferdinand

1   There be some Sports are painfull ; & their labor
    Delight in them [set] off : Some kindes of basenesse
    Are nobly undergon ; and most poore matters
    Point to rich ends : this my meane Taske
    Would be as heavy to me, as odious, but
    The Mistris which I serve, quickens what's dead,
    And makes my labours, pleasures : O She is
    Ten times more gentle, [then] her Father's crabbed ;
    And he's compos'd of harshnesse .

2   I must remove
    Some thousands of these Logs, and pile them up,
    Upon a sore injunction ; my sweet Mistris
    Weepes when she sees me worke, & saies, such basenes
    Had never like Executor : I forget :
    But these sweet thoughts, doe even refresh my labours,
    Most [busie lest], when I doe it .

Within the onrushed F #1, the four pieces of major punctuation in the first four lines and the four extra breath-thoughts that quickly follow all seem to mark just where Ferdinand's (probable) handling of the first

Act III, Scene i (Ferdinand, Miranda, Prospero) 91

menial task in his life requires extra effort, with the semicoloned moments perhaps requiring more effort than the others.

• And the occasional small cluster of unembellished words in the somewhat emotional (2/4) first three and half lines (" ; & their labor / Delight in them sets off : "; "Are nobly undergon"; "Point to rich ends"; "Would be as heavy to me, as odious"; "quickens what's dead") could well suggest a moment of rest before beginning the physical heavy work once again.

• It's possible that he stops the work to condemn "this my meane Taske" making his "labours, pleasures", for these next three lines are not interrupted by major punctuation and are also passionate (2/3).

• Then the comparison of Miranda ("ten times more gentle") to her father ("crabbed") is intellectual (3/1, F #1's last two lines), and highlighted by being set as emotional (semicolon-created) surround phrases.

• The relative care of F #2's first two lines (1/0) and the subject matter suggest that Ferdinand may have started his labors once more.

• However, recalling his "Mistris"'s tears and words move him to passion once more (2/2), and in finishing with the fact that he can "refresh" himself from "these sweet thoughts", he becomes totally emotional (0/3 the last two lines of the speech).

**MIRANDA   ALAS, NOW PRAY YOU / WORKE NOT SO HARD :
I WOULD THE LIGHTNING HAD BETWEEN**

Background: Defying her father's orders, Miranda has come to help Ferdinand. Unbeknownst to her, Prospero is watching over them both and is secretly delighted.

Style: As part of a two-handed scene.

Where: Near to Prospero's cell.

To Whom: Ferdinand, unaware that Prospero is watching.

# of Lines: 12   **Probable Timing:** 0.40 minutes

Miranda

1   Alas, now pray you
   Worke not so hard : I would the lightning had
   Burnt up those Logs that you are enjoynd to pile :
   Pray set it downe, and rest you : when this burnes

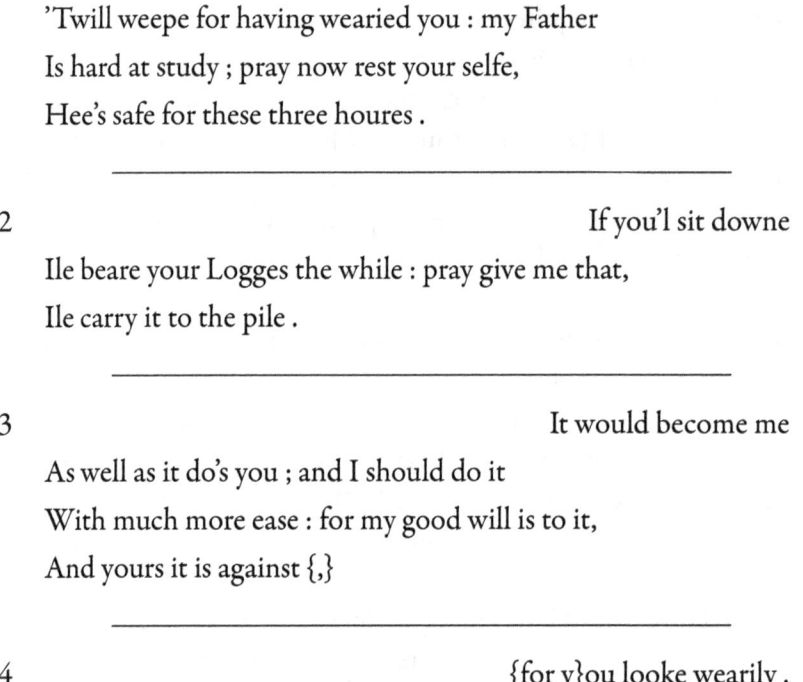

'Twill weepe for having wearied you : my Father
Is hard at study ; pray now rest your selfe,
Hee's safe for these three houres .

———————————————————

2   If you'l sit downe
Ile beare your Logges the while : pray give me that,
Ile carry it to the pile .

———————————————————

3   It would become me
As well as it do's you ; and I should do it
With much more ease : for my good will is to it,
And yours it is against {,}

———————————————————

4   {for y}ou looke wearily .

Given that this is her first teenage love situation, it's not surprising that the speech is emotional overall (3/12 in eleven and a half lines). What is startling is that all but the last phrase can be described as surround phrases. Also the eight pieces of major punctuation not only mark where she wants to make her thoughts absolutely clear, they also seem to set up moments where she's almost tongue-tied and not quite sure what to say next—especially at each point where the semicolons mark where she almost says much too much.

• The first sentence is carefully emotional (2/8) with essentially just one heightened word per phrase, and this together with the monosyllabic opening "Alas, now pray you / Worke not so hard : " suggests Miranda is very vulnerable both in words and feelings.

• Thus the two phrases with double releases, about the "Logs" ("when this burnes / 'Twill weepe for having wearied you") and her father ("Hee's safe for these three hours . "), probably carry extra weight as far as she (and may be Ferdinand) is concerned.

• The move from talking to him to actually physically helping him, F #2's " . If you'l sit downe / Ile beare your Logges the while : " is very strong, set as it is as a passionate monosyllabic surround phrase (1/3), so it's strange that the surround phrase that follows is unembellished—unless

Act III, Scene i (Ferdinand, Miranda, Prospero) 93

she either realizes that she may have said too much or perhaps even come too close to him physically.

- Whatever the reason, it has had a great impact on her—for the final three-and-a-half-line sentence is also totally unembellished, and it seems the calmness is very carefully enforced, for bubbling underneath her explanation is the start with two surround phrases start (created by the emotional semicolon), the second also monosyllabic.

FERDINAND   NOBLE MISTRIS, {ψ} I DO BESEECH YOU

Background: This is Ferdinand's response to Miranda's suggestion "You looke wearily", in which, upon at last learning her name, he starts his wooing by (perhaps rather clumsily) playing formal word games based upon her name, which he quickly abandons for straightforward honesty.

Style: As part of a two-handed scene.

Where: Near to Prospero's cell.

To Whom: Miranda, unaware that Prospero is watching

# of Lines: 28   **Probable Timing:** 1.30 minutes

Ferdinand

1   {ψ} Noble Mistris, {ψ} I do beseech you
     Cheefely, that I might set it in my prayers,
     What is your name ?

---

2   Admir'd Miranda,
     Indeede the top of Admiration, worth
     What's deerest to the world : full many a Lady
     I have ey'd with best regard, and many a time
     Th'harmony of their tongues, hath into bondage
     Brought my too diligent eare : for severall vertues
     Have I lik'd severall women, never any
     With so full soule, but some defect in her
     Did quarrell with the noblest grace she ow'd,
     And put it to the foile .

3   But you, O you,

So perfect, and so peerelesse, are created
Of everie Creatures best .

---

4   I am, in my condition

    A Prince (Miranda) I do thinke a King
    (I would not so) and would no more endure
    This wodden slaverie, [then] to suffer
    The flesh-flie blow my mouth : heare my soule speake.

5   The verie instant that I saw you, did
    My heart flie to your service, there resides
    To make me slave to it, and for your sake
    Am I this patient Logge-man .

6   O heaven ; O earth, beare witnes to this sound,
    And crowne what I professe with kinde event
    If I speake true : if hollowly, invert
    What best is boaded me, to mischiefe : I,
    Beyond all limit of what else i'th world
    Do love, prize, honor you .

---

7   Wherefore weepe you ?

This is another fine example of a teenager in love, and what is remarkable about it is that after the opening flailing (9/15 in the eighteen lines of F #1–4), the moment he speaks of "The verie instant that I saw you", five of the final ten lines are unembellished, in part suggesting that his attempted rhetorical game playing and embarrassment are over—but his feelings are not, for the remaining six lines are full of emotional release (0/6).

• Thus Ferdinand starts very carefully, with the beginning of the first and second lines each showing a little release, and then finding some self-control for the remainder of each line and the monosyllabic unembellished key question "What is your name?"—so far having only been able to refer to her as his "Mistris".

• Learning her name allows him to spring into a small series of passionate dreadful word games (3/2, the first four lines of F #2), though

Act III, Scene i (Ferdinand, Miranda, Prospero)   95

he becomes very quiet (an enforced calm?) as he offers the word-sound match of "full many a Lady / I have ey'd".

• And then, whether he is immediately conscious of it, expanding his earlier mention of "full many a Lady" to stating he has admired "severall women" arouses emotion in him (0/5 the five and a half lines ending the sentence).

• And, as he turns his attention to "you, O you", he becomes passionate (2/1, F #3).

• His intellectual definition (3/1, the first line that opens F #4) of himself as "King", quickly undercut by the unembellished sad, oblique reference to the presumed death of his father ("I would not so"), then turns to emotion (0/4, the last three lines of F #4) as the sentence ends with his emotional monosyllabic surround phrase plea to " : heare my soule speake . ")

• Then comes an unembellished passage of nearly four lines as he explains it is only because "My heart flie to your service" that he is putting up with being a "Logge-man" (the only words that break the calm, F #5, 1/1).

• Not surprisingly, his appeal for "heaven" and "earth" to "witness" what he is about to say is highly emotional (1/7, F #6's first four lines), while, quite charmingly, the final two-line declaration that "I . . . love, prize, honor you" is completely unembellished.

• And then comes the wonderful, and again charming, teenage lack of understanding as he innocently poses the last very short question: "Wherefore weepe you?" (F #7, 0/1)

MIRANDA   I DO NOT KNOW / ONE OF MY SEXE ; NO WOMANS FACE REMEMBER,

Background: And this is Miranda's response to Ferdinand's love declaration (the prior speech). Since she has had no experience of playing coy (compare Juliet's lovely admission to Romeo: "I should have beene more strange, I must confesse"), she is as innocently open, direct, and honest as she is elsewhere in the play.

Style: As part of a two-handed scene.

Where: Near to Prospero's cell.

To Whom: Ferdinand, unaware that Prospero is watching.

# of Lines: 21   **Probable Timing:** 1.10 minutes

Miranda

1   I do not know

    One of my sexe ; no womans face remember,

    Save from my glasse, mine owne : Nor have I seene
    More that I may call men, [then] you good friend,
    And my deere Father : how features are abroad
    I am skillesse of ; but by my modestie
    (The jewell in my dower) I would not wish
    Any Companion in the world but you :
    Nor can imagination forme a shape
    Besides your selfe, to like of : but I prattle
    Something too wildely, and my Fathers precepts
    I therein do forget .

---

2   I am a foole
    To weepe at what I am glad of .

---

3   {And I weepe }
    At mine unworthinesse, that dare not offer
    What I desire to give ; and much lesse take
    What I shall die to want : But this is trifling,
    And all the more it seekes to hide it selfe,
    The bigger bulke it shewes .
4   Hence bashfull cunning,
    And prompt me plaine and holy innocence .
5   I am your wife, if you will marrie me ;
    If not, Ile die your maid : to be your fellow
    You may denie me, but Ile be your servant
    Whether you will or no .

In comparison to most modern texts' rational nine sentences, F's five sentences seem to present a character with much less self-control—yet by speech's end, F's orthography has marked Miranda's wonderful growth from awkwardness to maturity, a far more interesting and truthful human reality for a young adolescent in love than the self-controlled young woman the modern reworking seems to present.

Act III, Scene i (Ferdinand, Miranda, Prospero) 97

• That Miranda finds her I-don't-know-what-men-and-women-are-like opening quite awkward can be seen in that:
  a) F sets the confession as one onrushed sentence;
  b) there are four pieces of major punctuation in the first five lines;
  c) three of the four surround phrases so created are emotional, formed in part by semicolons; and
  d) the whole is quite emotional (2/6).

• And, as she asserts by the "jewell" of her "modestie" she "would not wish / Any Companion in the world but you", she seems to establish self-control, for in the ensuing four lines only three operative words are singled out for release, (as already seen, "jewell" and "Companion", accompanied by "your selfe"), all three vital to her own declaration of love, the latter heightened by being set in a surround phrase.

• And, as charmingly as with Ferdinand's awkwardness, her confession that she prattles "Something too wildely" is also set as a surround phrase where emotion and intellect both break into her self-control (1/1, the last two lines of F #1).

• And then her emotions take over and she voices thoughts of her own "unworthinesse" and acknowledges her tears (1/9, F #2–3. This is especially noticeable in the only (emotional) surround phrase in the sentence, " ; and much lesse take / What I shall die to want ; ", its pain heightened by being monosyllabic.

• Yet, a great testament to her inner fortitude, following her emotional rejection of "bashfull cunning" and her plea for the help of "holy innocence" (F #4, 0/2), is the final three-and-a-half-line declaration of complete love, which is totally unembellished, the first declarations once more formed by two emotional surround phrases.

Act III, Scene ii: Modern Text

CALIBAN Be not afeard; the isle is full of noises,°
Sounds and sweet airs, that give delight and hurt not.
Sometimes a thousand twangling instruments   130
Will hum about mine ears; and sometime voices
That, if I then had waked after long sleep,
Will make me sleep again; and then, in dreaming,
The clouds methought would open and show riches
Ready to drop upon me, that when I waked,   135
I cried to dream again.

Act III, Scene ii (Caliban)

music, sounds

128–38 Caliban's concern for Stephano is unexpectedly gentle; his master had denied being "afeard," but Caliban can recognize fear when he sees it. To reassure him, he talks of the island's music with great delicacy, his words sustained by gentle and lulling rhythms until he remembers his tears at the loss of all delight (l. 136). At the touch of fear, boisterous comedy and ferocious talk have yielded to rapt attention.

Caliban's description of enchantment and dreams is a climactic and effective opportunity for the actor to emphasize the gentler and more responsive aspects of Caliban and his independence. In the structure of the play, it is significant as one of series of incidents in which characters show the nature and strength of their imaginations. Alonso, Gonzalo, Ferdinand and Miranda have already done so. Prospero will call for a masque in the next Act to represent his own "present fancies" (IV.i.122) and then liken all human experience to such a dream. The delight, power and insecurity of imaginary "reality" are thus made evident, and also its dangers: Prospero, for example, abruptly ends the masque (see IV.i.139) because he remembers the practical necessity of coping with Caliban's conspiracy.

Act III, Scene ii: First Folio Speech

CALIBAN   BE NOT AFFEARD, THE ISLE IS FULL OF NOYSES,

Background: Unbeknownst to the conspirators, Ariel has been listening to Caliban's attempt to enlist Stephano and Trinculo in his plot to kill Prospero. Trying to distract them, Ariel starts to play back to them the tune of the aggressive catch of attack that they have been singing in celebration. Since he is invisible, Trinculo and Stephano become very alarmed, and thus, in the following, Caliban tries to reassure them.

Style: As part of a three-handed scene.

Where: Somewhere on the island.

To Whom: Stephano and Trinculo, in front of the invisible Ariel.

# of Lines: 9   **Probable Timing:** 0.30 minutes

Caliban

1   Be not affeard, the Isle is full of noyses,
Sounds, and sweet aires, that give delight and hurt not :
Sometimes a thousand twangling Instruments
Will hum about mine eares ; and sometime voices,
That if I then had wak'd after long sleepe,
Will make me sleepe againe, and then in dreaming,
The clouds methought would open, and shew riches
Ready to drop upon me, that when I wak'd
I cri'de to dreame againe .

With modern texts splitting F's onrushed single sentence in two, their speech becomes a matter of explanation: the original F setting allows Caliban to be caught up in his reverie from the start, the two extra breath thoughts allowing for extra details of delight.

- The opening overall description is passionate (2/4 the first three and a half lines), and then Caliban becomes emotional as the longing between waking and dreaming is expanded upon (0/6, the last five lines).

- The surround phrase " : Sometimes a thousand twangling Instruments / Will hum about mine eares ; ", created in part by the emotional semicolon, seems to point to the most wondrous of what the isle has to offer.

Act III, Scene ii (Caliban)

- Generally, the few releases tend to come in small clusters, as "the Isle is full of noyses" (1/1); "Will make me sleepe againe" (0/2); and "I cri'de to dreame againe" (0/3).

Act IV, Scene i: Modern Text

PROSPERO *[Aside]* I had forgot that foul conspiracy
Of the beast Caliban and his confederates   140
Against my life. The minute of their plot
Is almost come. *[To the Spirits]* Well done! Avoid!° No more!

FERDINAND This is strange. your father's in some passion°
That works° him strongly.

MIRANDA Never till this day
Saw I him touch'd with anger so distempered.°   145

PROSPERO You do look, my son, in a moved sort,°
As if you were dismayed. Be cheerful, sir.
Our revels° now are ended. These our actors,
As I foretold you, were all spirits and
Are melted into air, into thin air;   150
And, like the baseless° fabric° of this vision,
The cloud-capped towers, the gorgeous palaces,
The solemn temples, the great globe itself,
Yea, all which it inherit,° shall dissolve
And, like this insubstantial pageant faded,   155
Leave not a rack° behind. We are such stuff
As dreams are made on; and our little life
Is rounded° with a sleep. Sir, I am vexed.
Bear with my weakness; my, brain is troubled:

Act IV, Scene i (Prospero, Ferdinand, Miranda)

139–145 As Prospero's masque and celebration is about to reach its climax, Prospero unexpectedly steps onto the stage-within-the-stage and, suddenly, everything stops.

go away

deep feeling
affects, moves

While he speaks, Prospero probably holds his staff aloft, causing everyone on stage to be frozen in their various positions, "spell-stopped". At the end of line 142, he orders the masquers away and with a "confused noise" (echoing the sound of the shipwreck), they all "heavily vanish." Prospero is left alone at center-stage, torn by his passion (see l. 143), too angry for further words. Miranda says, quite specifically, that he has never looked like this before (see ll. 144-45). The play itself seems to founder, like a ship driven on rocks at sea; and it is clear that this destructive impulse has sprung from Prospero's own mind.

troubled, out of temper
agitated state of mind

entertainment

without foundation
building / contrivance

In the aftermath, Ferdinand and Miranda comment apprehensively, but they cannot speak to Prospero or offer any assistance. Both are deeply affected and disturbed (see ll. 146-47).

occupy it

mist, cloud (pun on *wrack*,
 a spelling of wreck)
completed

146–63 Although passionately involved (see ll. 144-145), Prospero speaks gently to Ferdinand, as if concerned chiefly for him. At first he talks simply about the end of their "revels," as if it were to be expected. But he is drawn into his explanation, so that he remembers all the glories of the world along with the "baseless" fiction of his own most hopeful "fancies." His speech has energy and commanding authority, but also a number of dying falls that become increasingly effective until he speaks of a "little life" and its completion in a sleep that sounds painless. It can be spoken in contrasting ways: Prospero may regret the loss of all that is "gorgeous" and "solemn," wishing he could dream for ever; or he can devalue these seductive notions because they are insubstantial vanities. The rhythms and versification are best suited to the former interpretation.

Be not disturbed with my infirmity. 160
If you be pleased, retire into my cell,
And there repose. A turn or two I'll walk,
To still my beating mind.

Ferdinand/Miranda We wish you peace.

Act IV, Scene i (Prospero, Ferdinand, Miranda)

After the philosophizing, rhythms change again as Prospero concludes by apologizing for himself and his "weakness," and by caring for Ferdinand's peace of mind. Abrupt phrases suggest, however, that Prospero's thoughts are now elsewhere; he may start walking "a turn or two" (l. 162) already.

Before leaving the stage, the young couple speak together, very simply, wishing Prospero the "peace" which obviously he had not yet regained after the "strong" working of his passion. They do not respond to what he has just said, but rather retreat in the face of obvious signs of suffering and a "beating" mind (l. 163).

Act IV, Scene i: First Folio Speech

PROSPERO I HAD FORGOT THAT FOULE CONSPIRACY

Background: With two of three matters of concern in hand if not completely resolved (the betrothal of Miranda and Alonso's son, Ferdinand, and the controlling of his old Milanese and Neapolitan adversaries), there is still one major concern outstanding, which causes Prospero to interrupt the glorious musical and visual masque being offered by Ariel and the spirits to celebrate the betrothal.

Style: Intially as a group interruption, then as part of a three-handed scene, finally as a two-handed scene.

Where: Wherever on the island the betrothal celebration Masque is being held.

To Whom: Initially the group as a whole—spirits including Ariel, Juno, Ceres and Iris and the humans Miranda and Ferdinand; then just the two humans; finally Ariel alone.

# of Lines: 24 **Probable Timing:** 1.15 minutes

Prospero

1 I had forgot that foule conspiracy
   Of the beast Calliban, and his confederates
   Against my life : the minute of their plot
   Is almost come : Well done, avoid : no more .

---

2 You doe looke (my son) in a mov'd sort,
   As if you were dismaid : be cheerefull Sir,
   Our Revels now are ended : These our actors,
   (As I foretold you) were all Spirits, and
   Are melted into Ayre, into thin Ayre,
   And like the baselesse fabricke of this vision
   And Clowd-capt Towres, the gorgeous Pallaces,
   The solemne Temples, the great Globe it selfe,
   Yea, all which it inherit, shall dissolve,

Act IV, Scene i (Prospero, Ferdinand, Miranda)

> And like this insubstantiall Pageant faded
> Leave not a racke behinde : we are such stuffe
> As dreames are made on ; and our little life
> Is rounded with a sleepe : Sir, I am vext,
> Beare with my weakenesse, my old braine is troubled :
> Be not disturb'd with my infirmitie,
> If you be pleas'd, retire into my Cell,
> And there repose, a turne or two, Ile walke
> To still my beating minde .

---

3   Come with a thought : I thank thee Ariell : come .
[Enter Ariell]

---

4   Spirit : We must prepare to meet with Caliban .

- The urgent thought that has interrupted him is highlighted by the final surround phrases of F #1—": the minute of their plot / Is almost come : Well done, avoid : no more ."—and those of F #3–4 that end the speech: " . Come with a thought : I thank thee Ariell : come . / Spirit : We must prepare to meet with Caliban ."
- Noticing the shock that his interruption has given to Ferdinand (if not Miranda too) he comments in another surround phrase, ": be cheerefull Sir, / Our Revels now are ended ."
- While both his philosophy and confusion are highlighted in a third passage of three successive surround phrases, the opening philosophy heightened by being expressed in part via the only (emotional) semicolon in the speech—": we are such stuffe / As dreames are made on ; and our little life / Is rounded with a sleepe : Sir, I am vext, / Beare with my weakenesse, my old braine is troubled :"—followed by the very quiet (pleading?), unembellished "Be not disturb'd with my infirmitie," which, coupled with the later comment in Act Five of "Every third thought shall be my grave," may have more significance for Prospero than his listeners may comprehend.

- The speech opens powerfully (1/2, the first one-and-a-half lines), and then, via the surround phrases, Prospero evinces some momentary control (1/0 to the end of F #1).

- The attempt to calm Ferdinand and the explanation of how "Our Revels now are ended" that opens F #2's first six lines are passionate (5/7), and, while the initial description of the edifices continues passionately (5/4 the next two lines), so as the "Globe it selfe" is mentioned there comes the hushed "Yea, all which it inherit, shall dissolve" before an emotional conclusion covering both the thought "we are such stuffe / As dreames are made on" and the admission that his "braine" is "troubled" (2/9 the next five lines to the final colon of F #2).

- And he may be tired (hardly surprising, considering the magic he has initiated already throughout the play), for apart from the emotional idea that "a turne or two, Ile walke / To still my beating minde," the remaining six lines of the speech are passionate but quieter (4/3), though the F #3–4 surround phrases that end the speech underscore that he very clearly understands how much he has left to do.

www.ingramcontent.com/pod-product-compliance
Lightning Source LLC
Chambersburg PA
CBHW080552170426
43195CB00016B/2762